"William Boekestein's 1
This is a 'once-over'—a survey of the whole field of eschatology—yet it doesn't treat the topics lightly. In addition to discussing our Lord's return and the millennium, Boekestein addresses death and dying, the intermediate state, as well as the nature of heaven. He includes a very helpful discussion of the kingdom of God as well when he addresses how our views on eschatology should inform our understanding of the church's mission. I highly recommend it for personal use (and even devotions) as well as church study groups interested in the topic. Well done, Rev. Boekestein!"

—Kim Riddlebarger, senior pastor at Christ Reformed Church in Anaheim (URCNA), cohost of the *White Horse Inn*, and visiting professor of systematic theology at Westminster Seminary California

"William Boekestein has served the church well by writing *The Future of Everything*. Anyone looking for a primer on eschatology will discover an excellent resource in these pages. Boekestein addresses the range of subjects that fall under the heading of eschatology in an accessible and concise yet informative way. Most importantly, every Christian reading this little volume will find their eyes directed more toward heaven and their hearts stirred by the eternal promises of God."

—Jason Helopoulos, senior pastor at University Reformed Church

"Pastor Boekestein has written a simple but solid and, at times, searching guide to eschatology. This is not in any way a 'theoretical' book, but rather one that is immensely practical for all Christians. I personally think many will find this to be clear and compelling on topics of great importance."

—Mark Jones, pastor at Faith Vancouver PCA

"In the Bible and the early church, eschatology was the fundamental category of the gospel—the kingdom of God has come. But in many years in between, eschatology has been moved to the back burner as mere reflection on the future. In this book William Boekestein invites us to reconsider this marginalization of eschatology. Some eschatological vision will shape our understanding of the meaning of human life and missionary calling of the church today, and Boekestein calls us back to a biblical one. May God use this book to equip the church to live more and more in light of the present and coming kingdom of God."
—Michael W. Goheen, adjunct professor of missional theology, Covenant Theological Seminary

"This is definitely a book I'd give my friends who want to understand the end times from a biblical perspective. Grounded in Scripture, *The Future of Everything* is immensely practical—at least for everyone who will die one day. I heartily recommend it!"
—Michael Horton, J. Gresham Machen Professor of Theology, Westminster Seminary California

"Eschatology is practical. William Boekestein does every Christian a favor by treating this practical subject in such a practical and simple way. He manages to do this without being superficial. I highly recommend his little book."
—Sam Waldron, president of Covenant Baptist Theological Seminary

"A brief simple book on the end times? Is that possible? You have it in your hands, and with just a little effort you can soon have it in your head and heart. It will not only prepare you for the end but also equip you to prepare others for eternity."
—David Murray, professor of Old Testament and practical theology at Puritan Reformed Theological Seminary

"Here is a clear, orderly survey of what the Bible teaches us to expect as God works out His purpose for His world."

—J. I. Packer, Board of Governors' Professor of Theology, Emeritus, Regent College

"This volume succeeds admirably in presenting biblical teaching on the end times for a broad readership yet without sacrificing substance. It rescues 'eschatology' from becoming an abstract word by emphasizing throughout the relevance and practical implications of what will take place at Christ's return for the present life of Christians and the mission of the church in the world. The series of questions that accompany each chapter make it ideal for individual and group study."

—Richard B. Gaffin Jr., professor emeritus of biblical and systematic theology, Westminster Theological Seminary

"Here is a truly excellent guide to the Christian's blessed hope. William Boekestein begins with the principles that safely guide us through this minefield, then helps us to see what the Bible really says about our personal future and the future of the world. I especially love its closing chapters, which show us how these truths impact our lives in the world and the church. Enjoy the full menu—including the sobering reality of hell and the ecstasy of heaven! Here is a pastor inviting us to a soul-enriching study through a captivating book that is hard to put down."

—Conrad Mbewe, pastor of Kabwata Baptist Church, chancellor of African Christian University, Lusaka, Zambia

THE FUTURE OF EVERYTHING

THE FUTURE OF EVERYTHING

Essential Truths about the End Times

William Boekestein

Reformation Heritage Books
Grand Rapids, Michigan

Reformation Heritage Books
2965 Leonard St. NE
Grand Rapids, MI 49525
616–977–0889
orders@heritagebooks.org
www.heritagebooks.org

Printed in the United States of America
19 20 21 22 23 24/10 9 8 7 6 5 4 3 2 1

Library of Congress Cataloging-in-Publication Data

Names: Boekestein, William, author.
Title: The future of everything : essential truths about the end times / William Boekestein.
Description: Grand Rapids, Michigan : Reformation Heritage Books, 2019. | Includes
   bibliographical references.
Identifiers: LCCN 2018054873 (print) | LCCN 2019003859 (ebook) | ISBN
   9781601786883 (epub) | ISBN 9781601786876 (pbk. : alk. paper)
Subjects: LCSH: Eschatology. | End of the world.
Classification: LCC BT821.3 (ebook) | LCC BT821.3 .B638 2019 (print) | DDC
   236—dc23
LC record available at https://lccn.loc.gov/2018054873

To my brothers
Nate, Jeremy, John,
and the many other "Bible Study Men"
over the years—dear friends and
fellow anticipators of Jesus's glorious return.

Contents

Preface

The Anglican poet John Donne (1572–1631) was once ravished with a fever that he feared might kill him. From his sickbed he could hear the sounds of a funeral. In fact, his home was close enough to the church that he could hear the psalm sung by the congregation; as best he could, he joined in the singing. But the funeral bells affected him most. Later he wrote, "I hear this dead brother of ours, who is now carried out to his burial, to speak to me, and to preach my funeral sermon in the voice of these bells. In him, O God, thou hast accomplished to me even the request of [the rich man] to Abraham; thou hast sent one from the dead to speak unto me." Confronted by thoughts of his own mortality, Donne prayed to God that if his fever were fatal he would die, "drowned...in the blood of thy Son; and if I live longer, yet I may now die the death of the righteous, die to sin; which death is a resurrection to a new life."[1]

Donne's experience illustrates the benefit of reflecting on the end of life as we know it. Thinking about our end can help us live well—and die well. Especially in our day, with low infant mortality rates, long life spans, and a medical model that typically removes dying people from society, we need to seize—and sometimes create—opportunities to focus on our end. And if we

---

1. John Donne, *Devotions upon Emergent Occasions and Death's Duel* (New York: Random House, 1999), 100–101.

understand human death as a sign that even "the heavens will pass away," the whole world will be laid bare, and "all these things will be dissolved" (2 Peter 3:10–11), then we also need to give thought to the end of everything.

We need eschatology. With God's help, that snooty, foreign-sounding word can introduce to us a world of comfort, for this age and the age to come.

Thanks to Will Hesterberg and his ministry partners at ITEM (item.org) for inviting me to teach a modular course on eschatology at Mihael Starin Theological Seminary in Osijek, Croatia. While preparing those lectures I also preached through the themes of the last things in my home congregation, Immanuel Fellowship Church in Kalamazoo, Michigan. I have been greatly helped both by the input from beloved congregants during several sermon discussion meetings and by the spirited questions and conversations over these themes with the students in Croatia. An earlier form of some of these chapters appeared in the *Outlook*, the bimonthly publication of Reformed Fellowship, and are published here with permission.

I am extremely grateful for John "Jack" Jeffery's careful reading of the manuscript and his numerous grammatical, literary, and theological suggestions. Sue Verschoof also helped catch a number of typos. A special thanks to David, Jay, Joel, Steve, and the rest of the amazing team at Reformation Heritage Books. I am privileged to serve alongside excellent elders at Immanuel who have a vision for the church that extends beyond our congregation and who, therefore, generously encouraged me in this project.

Thank you Hazel, Mina, Evangelia, Asher, and especially Amy for helping to fill my life with love, joy, adventure, and anticipation as we journey together closer to that last day.

PART ONE

INTRODUCING ESCHATOLOGY

CHAPTER 1

Why Should I Study the End Times?

Eschatology, the study of the last things, is a fancy word for something we all already do. All of us think about the end. Yes, our culture and our fears push to the periphery thoughts of our death and the life hereafter. But count on it: at some point in your life, you are going to agonize over what will happen to you after you breathe your last. You can't attend a funeral—whether of a religious or nonreligious person—without hearing somebody's eschatology or their concept of what happens after death. We are all eschatologists. But that doesn't mean we always engage the end times well. In at least three ways we could go wrong in this most basic theological discipline.

First, we are tempted to engage in speculative eschatology. When end-times study is not rooted in Scripture, it becomes vain dreaming, the dogmatization of our wishes. In a time of unfathomable suffering and pain, Job asked his mostly well-meaning friends, "How then will you comfort me with empty nothings? There is nothing left of your answers but falsehood" (Job 21:34 ESV). When it comes to matters of eternal life and death we need more than "empty nothings." We need more than traditional religious rituals and mantras that suggest, sometimes superficially, that the best is yet to come. The effervescent goal of living a decent life falls pitifully short of guaranteeing a blessed eternity. Vague wishes of a better afterlife are impotent to deliver solid hope. Speculative eschatology is a sign of biblical illiteracy and spiritual immaturity. When it comes to the end times, we need to put childish ways behind us and listen to what God says.

Second, we should beware of argumentative eschatology. For some of us the very topic of the end times is off-putting because it can be such a contentious issue. Some of us have felt our Christianity questioned by those who have a different concept of the end. But surely God does not peel back the curtains of future history, giving us a glimpse into the staggering profundity of death and judgment or the glorious return of the King of Heaven that we might contend with other Christians over how things will work out. It is certainly possible—and necessary—to distinguish between two conflicting end-times views without needlessly blustering about the perceived superiority of one's own view.

Third, we must avoid *avoiding* eschatology. It sounds pious to say, "I don't think much about the last things. I know God is in control. I'll leave it up to Him."[1] Is eschatology even necessary? Isn't it enough to simply trust that God will work everything out in the end? Should we not approach this topic with the attitude of David, who said, "Neither do I concern myself with great matters, nor with things too profound for me" (Ps. 131:1)? In reality, Scripture teaches us to develop what some have called an "apocalyptic spirituality"[2] in which we so deeply sense the dawning of the age to come that we begin to realize its wonder in this present age. The apostle Peter captures in a single phrase Scripture's unified application of eschatology. In light of God's plan to dissolve and purify the cosmos he asks, "What manner of persons ought you to be in holy conduct and godliness?" (2 Peter 3:11).

---

1. For a reflection on modern apathy on eschatological themes, see Geerhardus Vos, *Redemptive History and Biblical Interpretation: The Shorter Writings of Geerhardus Vos*, ed. Richard B. Gaffin Jr. (Phillipsburg, N.J.: Presbyterian and Reformed, 1980), 317–19.

2. See, for example, Bernard McGinn, ed., *Apocalyptic Spirituality: Treatises and Letters of Lactantius, Adso of Montier-en-Der, Joachim of Fiore, the Franciscan Spiritualists, Savonarola*, The Classics of Western Spirituality: A Library of the Great Spiritual Masters (Mahwah, N.J.: Paulist Press, 1979).

With Peter, Jesus (Mark 13:35–37) and Paul (1 Thess. 5:6) call God's people to respond to the coming of the end with watchful sobriety. The same emphasis is found in Hebrews 10:25. Seeing "the Day approaching" ought to strengthen our hope, devote us to worship, and galvanize us in our expressions of love and good works. If Christ is returning, if His judgment will be eternal, and if hell is as terrible as heaven is delectable, then studying the end times is eminently practical. Those who lose sight of the end can become careless in their conduct and arrogant in their rejection of God (see 2 Peter 3:1–7). By contrast, a biblical eschatology provides a rationale for ethics that goes deeper than pragmatic concerns. With God's help eschatology can chill our blood at the thought of sin and judgment, and it can warm our hearts with God's gracious work of redemption.

God invites us to meditate on the future, not to speculate or altercate but to better share His perspective on this life and the life to come. And this is how we should study the topic. The way Scripture and the church's historic confessions teach eschatology is much more like gazing upon a dazzling sunset than analyzing and describing the chemical properties of the sun.[3] We need more than a skeletal, technical, clinical understanding of the end times. We need a robust eschatological vision that can invigorate us with the reality that God's last work will change everything and that the change has begun.

So how can a believing understanding of eschatology promote "holy conduct and godliness"? Here are ten answers, not to prove the validity of the study of the end times but to help us begin to praise God for the beauty of His promise to be with His people till the end (Deut. 31:6).

---

3. See especially the Belgic Confession of Faith (henceforth BC), article 37.

1. Eschatology Personalizes and Universalizes Our Understanding of the Future

The study of the last things is usually divided into two parts. The Bible teaches that the history of this age will one day come to an end (1 Peter 4:7). Moreover, this present age will not quietly spin itself out of existence; it will end in an epic crisis and the start of a new age (2 Peter 3:10–11). When we think about this crisis—the return of Christ, the last judgment, the realization of the kingdom, and the population of heaven and hell—we are studying general eschatology. General eschatology draws us into thinking about more than simply what will happen to me when I die.

But before the coming of this great crisis, most people will have experienced the end of this age through death. When we consider death, the continued existence of the soul, and the intermediate state into which the dead enter, we are engaged in individual eschatology. This discipline can help people who are overly focused on this present age to meditate on their personal eternity.

2. Eschatology Elucidates Christian Theology

Eschatology is not an isolated doctrine. The last things *can* be studied as a doctrinal unit, one of the six heads of sacred theology. But the doctrine is also "a lens through which we come to understand the whole system of Christian faith and practice."[4] Studying the last things is like getting to the end of a novel; the entire story begins to make sense. Abraham Kuyper noted that every other division of theology "left some question unanswered, to which eschatology should supply the answer."[5] For the doctrine of God eschatology shows the completion of His work and providence. For the doctrine of man it punctuates both the natural end of sin and God's work of restoration. For the doctrine

---

4. Michael Horton, *The Christian Faith* (Grand Rapids: Zondervan, 2011), 906.

5. Quoted in Louis Berkhof, *Systematic Theology* (Grand Rapids: Eerdmans, 1939), 665.

of Christ it exposits the full meaning of Jesus's words from the cross: "It is finished" (John 19:30). For the doctrine of salvation it reveals how the Spirit will finally help bring about the deliverance that He has been sent to guarantee (Eph. 1:13–14). Finally, for the doctrine of the church it previews the glorious end of God's people who are presently embroiled in spiritual conflict. The doctrine of the end times is not a segregated article of faith but the consummation of the Bible's teaching on everything.

3. Eschatology Interprets Redemptive History

If we think of world history as a four-act drama—creation, fall, redemption, and restoration—we see how eschatology helps us understand each act.[6] First, the end times helps us understand the full trajectory of creation. In the early chapters of Genesis we learn that God is not only infinitely creative but also deeply relational. The garden is a picture of God's desire to dwell with His people in the beauty of a flawless friendship. But from the vantage point of Eden, it is not abundantly clear where God's world is heading. Eschatology shows us how God leads His people from a garden to a city that is built around a beautiful and safe relationship with Him.

Second, concerning the fall, everyone can sense the brokenness of this present age. Our conflicts and tears, bodily deterioration, and the certainty of death make us groan (2 Cor. 5:1–3). But our groaning expresses more than our desire to escape our terrors or the aches and pains of our body. We also yearn to be "further clothed, that mortality may be swallowed up by life" (2 Cor. 5:4). Eschatology helps shape our groaning according to God's promise of a better life (2 Cor. 5:1–4).

Third, in this present age, God is carrying out a work of redemption. Christ has come into our world declaring peace and

---

6. See Timothy Keller, *The Prodigal God: Recovering the Heart of the Christian Faith* (New York: Penguin, 2008), 95–103.

pardon. He has offered His blessed body to satisfy the demands of the law's curse (Gal. 3:10). He invites us to believe in Him and share in the benefits of His saving work. He has been raised from the dead to assure us that death has been swallowed up in victory (1 Cor. 15:54). Eschatology helps us to rejoice in God's already-present gift of salvation while reserving abundant hope for the life to come.

Fourth, one day God will restore His fallen people. So that we don't become either too comfortable or despondent in this present age, God confronts us with "the glory which shall be revealed in us" (Rom. 8:18). Lest we dismiss this world as insignificant, Scripture insists that the coming, complete restoration will reflect a measure of continuity with this present age.

4. Eschatology Pinpoints Believers' Current Place in History

We daily experience the tension of living between two worlds or ages. The New Testament regularly speaks of two successive ages or systems: this age[7] (cf. Matt. 12:32; Rom. 12:2) or the present age (Gal. 1:4; 1 Tim. 6:17), and "that age" (Luke 20:35) or "the age to come" (Matt. 12:32; see also Eph. 1:21). Vos writes, "Believers live in the 'last days,' upon them 'the ends of the ages are come,' but 'the last day,' 'the consummation of the age,' still lies in the future.... The contrast between these ages is (especially with Paul) that between the evil and transitory, and the perfect and abiding."[8] Understanding our place on God's redemptive time line delivers us from false expectations of a utopian age divorced from Christ's second coming. It also helps banish nagging fears that "all things continue as they were from the beginning of creation" (2 Peter 3:4). We live in a time of labor, though we anticipate an eternal rest.

---

7. In many instances (e.g., Matt. 13:22; Rom. 12:2) the Greek *aion* is translated "world" but denotes less a place than an age or era and its spirit.

8. Vos, *Redemptive History*, 26, 28.

5. Eschatology Reinforces a Biblical View of Ecology

If this physical world is just a sinking ship or a vast wasteland waiting to be burned up with fire, with no correspondence to the coming age, then believers seem to have few compelling reasons to care for the environment.[9] If not only humans but also every square inch of God's creation informs us of God's pattern for the new heavens and the new earth, however, then we can be encouraged to care for the earth since it should be as special to us as it is to God.

6. Eschatology Offers Hope in Suffering

For the believer, reflection on heaven provides an eternal context for our pain. This is what Paul has in mind when he says, "For I consider that the sufferings of this present age are not worthy to be compared with the glory which shall be revealed in us" (Rom. 8:18). Jesus makes the same point with an illustration: "A woman, when she is in labor, has sorrow because her hour has come; but as soon as she has given birth to the child, she no longer remembers the anguish, for joy that a human being has been born into the world. Therefore you now have sorrow; but I will see you again and your heart will rejoice, and your joy no one will take from you" (John 16:21–22). The joy of restoration enables believers to face trials with unearthly contentment (see Heb. 12:2). Astoundingly, the Bible teaches that the joy we anticipate in glory actually begins to impinge our hearts even now. In the Gospels, especially in John, "the realities of the future life are so vividly and intensely felt to be existent in heaven and from there

---

9. See Francis Schaeffer, *Pollution and the Death of Man: The Christian View of Ecology* (Wheaton, Ill.: Tyndale, 1970); cf. Gale Z. Heide, "What Is New about the New Heaven and the New Earth? A Theology of Creation from Revelation 21 and 2 Peter 3," *Journal of the Evangelical Theological Society* 40, no.1 (March 1997): 37–56.

operative in the believer's life, that the distinction between what is now and what will be hereafter enjoyed becomes less sharp."[10]

7. Eschatology Moderates the Power of Politics

Every election cycle tempts us to either embrace the incoming leaders as messianic manifestations of God's salvation or cower before the new regime as a sure sign of the end of the world as we know it. A balanced eschatology assures us that our current leader is neither our savior nor one of the riders of the apocalypse, nor was the previous leader, nor will be the succeeding leader. Daniel's glimpse into the future contrasts the indestructible kingdom of the coming savior Jesus (Dan. 7:14) with the hosts of rulers whose kingdoms are now buried under ash and dust. Eschatology does not discourage us from political action, but it does keep our eyes fixed on the One whose kingdom will know no end (Luke 1:33).

8. Eschatology Urges Personal and Vocational Excellence

One of the main purposes of both of Paul's canonical letters to the Thessalonians was to correct the believers' faulty eschatology. Part of their error seems to have been a penchant for laziness since they reasoned, "Jesus is coming back; of what account is my work?" Paul invokes the returning Christ to urge these believers to "work in quietness and eat [your] own bread" (2 Thess. 3:12). Matthew Henry commented on Jacob's skill at the selective breeding of sheep in Genesis 30: "It becomes a man to be master of his trade, whatever it is, and to be not only industrious, but ingenious in it, and to be versed in all its lawful arts and mysteries."[11] The truth of this statement is magnified by the ongoing work of God in salvation and the consummation of His work promised in the doctrine of the last things.

---

10. Vos, *Redemptive History*, 28. Cf. BC 37.

11. Matthew Henry, *Commentary on the Whole Bible* (Old Tappan, N.J.: Fleming H. Revell, n.d), 1:183.

Peter says that when Christ returns we will be "found by Him" (2 Peter 3:14). Each of us will be doing something when we are found by God. No one should want to be found sinning either through laziness or any other vice. And we don't know when Christ will return (2 Peter 3:10). So since we will all appear before Christ and His judgment seat, "we make it our aim, whether present or absent, to be well pleasing to Him" (2 Cor. 5:9).

9. Eschatology Invigorates Missions and Evangelism

When Revelation shows us the redeemed in glory, we realize that they were saved through the witness of believers in this present age (Rev. 20:4). God is patient in sending Christ because He is "not willing that any should perish but that all should come to repentance" (2 Peter 3:9). When we share God's heart we will take up the Great Commission with new vigor. "The Church can be rightly understood only in an eschatological perspective…. The meaning of this 'overlap of the ages' in which we live, the time between the coming of Christ and his coming again, is that it is a time given for the witness of the apostolic Church to the ends of the earth…. The implication of a true eschatological perspective will be missionary obedience, and the eschatology which does not issue in such obedience is a false eschatology."[12]

10. Eschatology Grounds Us in Christ

The Old Testament emphasis on the end times is largely centered on the history of Israel. The big question is, What is the destiny of God's people? But the later prophets' increased focus on the individual masterfully prepares the way for the coming of Christ who, at the same time, fulfills the calling of Israel to "do justly, love mercy, and to walk humbly with your God" (Micah 6:8) and

---

12. Lesslie Newbigin, *The Household of God: Lectures on the Nature of the Church* (New York: Friendship Press, 1954), 153–54.

opens by His blood a new and living way for individuals to enter
into a restored life with God (Heb. 10:19–22). The last days began
with the first coming of Christ. The starkness of the contrast
between this present age and the age to come, between this world
and the next, was never as obvious as at the coming of Christ. To
think eschatologically is to think Christologically.

One final caution: we need to exercise biblical reserve when
we study the end times. The Bible hasn't said nearly enough
to satisfy the curiosity of the inquisitive. But it has said enough
about the end times to encourage us to study it. And when studied and believed, the doctrines of the last things can inspire us
with the joy, patience, and holiness of the One whose return we
eagerly await.

CHAPTER 2

How Can I Understand Prophecy?

All of us think about the end times. When we reflect on what will happen, not only when we die but when this present age ends, some combination of ideas, images, hopes, and fears floods our minds. And this is good. God wants us to reflect on the last things, to cultivate an apocalyptic spirituality in which our vision for the future impacts our walk before God's face today.

For that to happen well, our eschatology, our doctrine of the last things, needs to be drawn from Scripture and not simply reflect our prejudices or wishes. But when we study the last things, especially those things connected with the end of this present age and the beginning of the next, we have to engage prophecy, a genre of Scripture that presents a host of interpretive challenges. But we don't need to read the prophets unarmed.

To understand the prophets we need to study them through the grid of a biblical hermeneutic. *Hermeneutics* is the science of interpretation. And even if we have never used the word, we all have a hermeneutic. We all study the Bible with certain assumptions, following definite rules or at least impulses, even if we couldn't articulate them. This is why two people can read the same passage and arrive at very different ideas, especially when studying prophecy. It is for lack of a biblically informed hermeneutic that some visions of the end are so complicated or wildly speculative that the author's intent is completely corrupted. To better understand the Bible's portrayal of the end times, it is critical to think through a number of issues that we face when interpreting prophecy.

The Bible Is a Story of Redemption

Neither the Old nor New Testament prophets spoke of the future merely to tell about a few spectacular events beforehand. Instead, they were instilling a God-centered piety by means of the story of God's redemption in the past, present, and future.

Still, it is possible to lose sight of the big picture on account of scintillating or perplexing prophetic details. In fact, this happens all the time. In my in-laws' home hangs a large framed mosaic puzzle. Each piece contains several tiny scenic photographs. You could study that framed puzzle with your nose a few inches away from the glass to inspect the individual photos. But when you step back from the mosaic you realize the purpose of the individual images is to build a larger composition—in this case a map of the entire world.

Likewise, it is possible to study end-times images as tiny, isolated portals into the future. But when you read their words as part of a grander mosaic, you realize that they are telling a story that is meant to inspire confidence in the meticulously skillful, patient, saving work of God. Prophesies that have been fulfilled and promises still to be realized bolster our confidence that God will continue to take "one from a city and two from a family" and build a holy kingdom called Zion, made up of people from all nations (Jer. 3:14, 17).

God does record prophecy to "show His servants the things which must shortly take place" (Rev. 22:6; cf. Rev. 1:1). But these "things" must never be isolated from the grand story they are helping to tell. Dan McCartney and Charles Clayton write, "Prophecy encourages us regarding the future, not by giving us the news headlines in advance, but by pointing to our victorious God, who has already won the decisive *heavenly* battle."[1]

---

1. Dan McCartney and Charles Clayton, *Let the Reader Understand: A Guide to*

The Story Starts at the Beginning

When we think about the end times, we naturally think of Revelation. If we do consider the Old Testament we might include Daniel or other prophets. But long before the ministry of the apostle John or the later prophets, the Bible introduced themes that, perhaps unexpectedly, help inform our understanding of the end.

Think about how the concept of death seems to intrude on the otherwise serene beginning of God's story. In the Bible's second chapter, in the context of so much good (Gen. 1:31), God warned of the possibility of death (Gen. 2:17). In the third chapter animals died (Gen. 3:21).[2] In the fourth chapter people began to die. In the book of beginnings we hear about a place where the dead go called sheol (Gen. 37:35).[3] God told Abraham that when he died, he would go to his fathers in peace (Gen. 15:15), and at

---

Interpreting and Applying the Bible (Phillipsburg, N.J.: P&R, 2002), 233. Consider another illustration. Suppose, in order to run some errands, I decided to leave my young children home alone for a few hours. Before leaving I might say to them, "Dad will only be gone briefly. I have to pick up some things for our home from the post office, the grocery store, and the hardware store. If you work hard cleaning the house while I'm gone, I'll be here before you know it to play the game you have been asking about." My point in telling my children where I hoped to go was not so that they could argue about which store I would go to first, second, or third or so that they could speculate on the sort of items I would buy at each store. I told them my plans to assure them that I left for their good and that I would return soon. I hoped to encourage them to work hard in my absence and to anticipate a good evening when I came back. With similar goals God inspired the prophets with visions of the future.

2. That God killed animals to provide skins for Adam and Eve is insufficient to prove that this was the first death. "Calvin and most reformed theologians were of the opinion that eating meat was permitted to humans even before the flood and the fall.... The animal world had already been placed under human dominion in Genesis 1:28, an act that certainly includes, especially with respect to the fish of the sea, the right to kill and use animals. Immediately after the fall God Himself made garments of animal skins (3:21)." Herman Bavinck, *Reformed Dogmatics*, vol. 2, *God and Creation* (Grand Rapids: Baker Academic, 2004), 575.

3. The Hebrew word for "grave" in Genesis 37:35 is *sheol*. The term is simply transliterated in the ESV and NAS.

death, Abraham was "gathered to his people" (Gen. 25:8). After just a few pages we begin to wonder what happens to dead people. Are they gone forever? How will God answer the cry of the blood of those unjustly taken from the land of the living (Gen. 4:10)? What is sheol, where was Abraham gathered to, and will those resting in peace ever wake?

Or, consider the important end-times theme of the kingdom of God. The Old Testament tells us that God is a king (1 Sam. 12:12) who is establishing a vast kingdom. He began gathering kingdom citizens when He rescued Adam and Eve from the deadly effects of Satan's tricks. He has since been preserving a faithful seed from their posterity, adding those from every nation—slowly at first, then more rapidly after Pentecost. But one day, as Jesus taught us to pray, His kingdom will come (Matt. 6:10). He will return to earth, His people will reign with Him, and He will exercise "the kingdom of his power in all the world."[4]

Likewise, the Old Testament tells us that God will conquer death and build a kingdom of life through His Messiah (Deut. 18:15–19; Acts 3:17–26), who will bring about the day of the Lord (Joel 2:1, 11, 31; see also Dan. 7:10), adjudicate a final judgment (Mal. 3:1–7), and raise to life every deceased person to either shame (Isa. 66:5–6) or glory (Job 19:25–27). The message of the end is woven throughout the entire story, even its beginning. To understand the end we have to be students of the whole Bible.

The Prophets Were Masterful Storytellers

To understand the language of prophecy, we need to humbly and diligently wrestle with several literary features of prophecy.

The Prophets Used Language and Forms Suitable to Their Time

The symbolic language of the prophets can be challenging. But rather than being a hurdle it can actually be a great gift. Symbolic

---

4. Westminster Larger Catechism (henceforth WLC) 191.

language engages our interest and stirs our imagination. With richly figurative language Isaiah predicted, "There shall come forth a shoot from the stump of Jesse, and a branch from his roots shall bear fruit" (Isa. 11:1 ESV). The symbolism powerfully calls to mind ideas of revival, vibrancy, and organic fruitfulness. Likewise, the robust symbolism of Revelation draws us into the story and floods our minds with powerful images of Christ's victory over evil. We should give thanks for apocalyptic symbolism and allow the context to determine when prophetic language should be taken literally.

Especially with prophesies that will be fulfilled in the far future, we should expect that the forms of the prophets' ideas might "have undergone radical changes" though their "essential central idea" will still be realized.[5] For example, when Ezekiel prophesied that a restored people would worship God on His holy hill, it is perfectly fitting for him to describe this end-times revival in terms of the construction of a temple (Ezekiel 40–48). In doing so, he follows a form long established in the construction of the tabernacle after the peoples' new birth from Egypt. But it is too simplistic to insist that the *form* of Ezekiel's prophecy might not change by the time of its fulfillment. Pastor and scholar Sidney Greidanus writes, "This historically and culturally conditioned form is completely overlooked when people in all seriousness propose that the prophets predict for our time a rebuilding of the temple in Jerusalem and reinstitution of animal sacrifices and a final battle fought with horses and chariots

---

5. Louis Berkhof, *Principles of Biblical Interpretation* (Grand Rapids: Baker, 1950), 151. Interacting with this question, Bernard Ramm explains that even a literalistic approach to prophesy "requires a measure of modulation," especially "in the interpretation of apocalyptic imagery a complete literalistic method is impossible." *Protestant Biblical Interpretation*, 3rd rev. ed. (Grand Rapids: Baker, 1970), 255, 268. Ramm urges caution as interpreters "proceed from the prophecy to its *manner* of fulfilment," 251.

and spears and swords."[6] God's word is never broken (John 10:35) though the form of its fulfillment can change.

Through the use of sometimes abstract language and impermanent forms, the prophets always communicated a central message. For example, in portraying a wolf grazing with a lamb (Isa. 65:25), Isaiah seems concerned not mainly to draw our attention to new feeding patterns of carnivores in a future age, but to the other-worldly peace that will characterize the age to come.

The Prophets Tell Stories in Layers

Students of prophecy often wonder whether certain predictions have been fulfilled already or if they have yet to be realized. Very often, the answer is, "Yes!" The prophets' messages frequently featured multiple layers in which "the earlier fulfillment is itself prophetic of the later fulfillment."[7] Remember, the entire story only finds its ultimate filling at the end. So Joel's prediction that someday God's Spirit would powerfully move His people to prophesy *and that* the earth, moon, and heavens would be violently disturbed (Joel 2:28–32) was realized at Pentecost (Acts 2), but not completely. Pentecost itself is a harbinger for the mighty stirring of the Spirit at "the coming of the great and awesome day of the LORD" (Joel 2:31).

Or, consider Jesus's end-times speech in Mark 13. Rather than insisting that the entire discourse was fulfilled by the Roman invasion of AD 70, or that it *only* points to the end of the age (or dissecting the passage into the parts that purportedly only

---

6. Sidney Greidanus, *The Modern Preacher and the Ancient Text: Interpreting and Preaching Biblical Literature* (Grand Rapids: Eerdmans, 1981), 232. It is important to insist that while Scripture texts have a single sense, they might have multiple fulfillments. As Ramm explains, "If the Scriptures had many meanings interpretation would be equivocal, but manifold fullfilment of a generic prophesy preserves the one sense of Scripture. Both promises and threats work themselves out over a period of time and therefore may pass through several fulfillments. Or one may view the same event from more than one perspective." *Protestant Biblical Interpretation*, 252–53.

7. McCartney and Clayton, *Let the Reader Understand*, 234.

speak to either event), "It might be simpler to take the whole as immediately, but partially…fulfilled in the Jewish War, but also to recognize that the events of that war point forward to the end of history."[8] Has Martin Luther King's dream from 1963 been fulfilled, "that one day…little black boys and black girls will be able to join hands with little white boys and white girls as sisters and brothers"? Yes, and no. Partly, but not perfectly. So it often is with biblical prophecy.

The Prophets Spoke to an Original Audience

The prophets were primarily preachers.[9] As watchmen (Ezek. 3:17) and shepherds (Jer. 3:15) they urged God's people to return to Him so that He might heal their backslidings and deliver them from His judgments and give them rest in His good land. They were surgeons who dissected the hearts of God's people to expose their disease and refer them to the Good Physician. "The prophets had, first of all, a message for their contemporaries. They were watchmen on the walls of Zion, to guide the destinies of the ancient people of God, and to guard against the dangers of apostasy."[10] For this reason, many prophesies are contingent on the actions of people. Through the prophets, God says, "If you… then I…" (Jer. 15:19, for example).

All Scripture, including prophecy, is "profitable for doctrine, for reproof, for correction, for instruction in righteousness, that the man of God may be complete, thoroughly equipped for every good work" (2 Tim. 3:16–17). God doesn't give us prophecy so that we can build elaborate time lines or speculate on the precise manner in which God will keep His word. He speaks about our future so that we will live faithfully in the present. He speaks to the contemporary audience to develop in us a robust vision for the end.

---

8. McCartney and Clayton, *Let the Reader Understand*, 235.
9. Greidanus, *The Modern Preacher*, 228.
10. Berkhof, *Principles*, 149.

The Story Is All about Jesus

If we are tempted to focus on the more mysterious, futuristic parts of biblical prophecy we should remember that at its core, the prophetic message was "always centered in the Kingdom of God, or the work of redemption through Christ."[11] When Paul was on trial for preaching a message of repentance to the Gentiles he told his judge that "to this day I stand, witnessing both to small and great, saying no other things than those which the prophets and Moses said would come—that the Christ would suffer, that He would be the first to rise from the dead, and would proclaim light to the Jewish people and to the Gentiles" (Acts 26:22–23). Jesus Himself said, "For assuredly, I say to you that many prophets and righteous men desired to see what you see, and did not see it, and to hear what you hear, and did not hear it" (Matt. 13:17). Peter echoed Jesus when he said, "Of this salvation the prophets have inquired and searched carefully, who prophesied of the grace that would come to you" (1 Peter 1:10). Twice on their way to Jerusalem, Jesus told His disciples that He would be betrayed and suffer body-and-soul-rending grief before rising from the dead (Luke 9:21–22, 43–45). When they could not understand what He was saying, Jesus marshaled the testimony of the prophets. "Behold, we are going up to Jerusalem, and all things that are written by the prophets concerning the Son of Man will be accomplished" (Luke 18:31).

Still the disciples missed the prophets' focus on God's promise to secure the kingdom through His suffering Servant. If the entire prophetic ministry revolved around the future comings of Christ, why did almost no one—including the apostles—get it when He came? It can be rightly said that only a small percentage of Old Testament prophesies *explicitly* "describe the Messiah or even the new covenant era."[12] But when taken as a whole, as they began to

---

11. Berkhof, *Principles*, 149.

12. Daniel M. Doriani, *Getting the Message: A Plan for Interpreting and Applying the Bible* (Phillipsburg, N.J.: P&R, 1996), 232.

be fulfilled, and especially after the Holy Spirit was poured out, Christ began to shine through every prophecy (John 12:16; 13:7, 19; 16:12–13). After the outer prophetic layers had been peeled back, Peter could preach, "But those things which God foretold by the mouth of all His prophets, that the Christ would suffer, He has thus fulfilled" (Acts 3:18). Significantly, when the New Testament speaks of the ministry of the prophets, it almost uniformly focuses on how they foretold the person and work of the Messiah. When we read prophecy, we need to understand that the message, while ostensibly about future events, is most essentially about God and His saving work through Christ.[13] It is not coincidental that the book of Revelation begins with a heart-stopping vision of Jesus ministering among the churches (Revelation 1–4) and ends with His promise to come back soon (Rev. 22:7, 12–13, 20).

The Story Concludes with a Revelation

When we study the end times, we tend to think about the book of Revelation. As we've seen, John's Revelation is only one of the many places in Scripture that give us a vision of the future. But it is a critically important prophetic book.

How Should We Study Revelation?

William Hendriksen has argued that John's Revelation consists of seven sections that each span the entire time period from Christ's first coming to His second coming, with each section generally moving toward the climax of history. In other words, the book is not arranged in strictly successive chronological fashion as one might expect. And yet, as the book progresses, especially starting at chapter twelve, God increasingly reveals the deeper spiritual battles that the church faces in this present age. The book is like a movie that returns seven times to the opening scene and records

---

13. See Greidanus, *The Modern Preacher*, 229.

the same story from a different angle, retelling the plot with increasing depth.[14]

What Does Revelation Teach Us?

Revelation itself prevents us from charting out a continuous history of successive events that will yet come to pass. John's apocalypse should not be read like a codebook that can be unlocked to tell the details of tomorrow's news today. Instead, we should read it as God's encouragement to a marginalized people. Despite the dark forces of evil and our own flagrant weaknesses, Christ will ever be among His people, leading them to victory against their mutual enemies. Through its masterful use of words and images, Revelation drives home this much-needed exhortation: he who, by faith in the Son of God, overcomes the trials of this life will not be disappointed by his reward in the life to come.

God's Word encourages us to study prophecy. We will sometimes puzzle over the prophets' use of unfamiliar symbols. We will not always be able to determine beyond doubt which events have been fulfilled and which are awaiting fulfillment. We cannot possibly presume to know with precision how God will bring His promises to pass. But in prophecy we can see God as the supreme storyteller whose word "calls those things which do not exist as though they did" (Rom. 4:17) and who exists as comfortably in the future as He does in the present and the past. Through prophecy He says to us, "Fear not, for I have redeemed you; I have called you by your name; you are Mine. When you pass through the waters, I will be with you; and through the rivers, they shall not overflow you. When you walk through the fire, you shall not be burned, nor shall the flame scorch you. For I am the LORD your God, the Holy One of Israel, your Savior" (Isa. 43:1–3).

---

14. William Hendriksen, *More than Conquerors: An Interpretation of the Book of Revelation* (Grand Rapids: Baker, 1998).

PART TWO

PERSONAL ESCHATOLOGY

CHAPTER 3

We're All Going to Die

The seventeenth-century Puritans and their more contemporary heirs commonly wrote about the four last things: death, judgment, heaven, and hell. Earlier audiences were rightly concerned about their future and wanted to learn about their looming eternity. Today, these topics have largely fallen out of favor, eclipsed by subjects that focus more explicitly on the here and now.

Still, in spite of our aversion to talking or thinking about death and what follows, we continue to die.

Isaac Watts's paraphrase of Psalm 90 puts it well:

> The busy tribes of flesh and blood,
> With all their lives and cares,
> Are carried downward by [God's] flood,
> And lost in following years.

> Time, like an ever-rolling stream,
> Bears all its sons away;
> They fly forgotten, as a dream
> Dies at the op'ning day.[1]

And, as always, death brings judgment (Heb. 9:27) and an eternity in heaven or hell. Unless Christ returns first, everyone who has ever lived will die. Death is disturbingly relevant.

---

1. *Trinity Psalter Hymnal* (Willow Grove, Pa.: Trinity Psalter Hymnal Joint Venture, 2018), 222.

With the subject of death, we begin to study individual eschatology, or the study of the last things for individuals prior to the
end of all things. We need a realistic, hopeful, and biblical perspective on death and how to process our own end and the deaths
of those around us.

The Idea of Death

From mere observation, we know death aborts ordinary life. But
to understand death beyond what we can see, we need divine
revelation.

Death is the antithesis of life, the foil of the beautiful portrait
painted in Genesis 2:7. In death God draws back to Himself and,
until the final judgment, keeps safe the spirits which animate our
material frame, while our physical bodies decay and return to the
elements from which they were formed (Eccl. 3:18–21; 12:6–7).
Louis Berkhof puts it succinctly: "Physical death is a termination
of physical life by the separation of body and soul." Still, Scripture
insists that "death is not a cessation of existence, but a severance
of the natural relations of life."[2] Death is contrary to nature.

And yet, like the stunted perspective of a person who has
never traveled beyond the limits of his blighted, boarded-up city,
death and decay seem normal to us. Since everything we observe
breaks down over time, it is easy to assume that death has always
been built in to life, a sort of planned obsolescence to promote
progress in the human race.

But the Bible insists that human death is a curse. God warned
the first humans that they would forfeit life if they disobeyed
His holy will (Gen. 2:17). When Adam violated God's command
against eating the fruit of the Tree of the Knowledge of Good
and Evil, he tested God's integrity and found it intact. He and
everyone connected to him by covenant headship—his wife and

---

2. Louis Berkhof, *Systematic Theology* (Grand Rapids: Eerdmans, 1939), 668.

his natural seed—began to die.[3] To use James's language, Adam's desire conceived and gave birth to sin, which always results in death (James 1:15). Paul sums it up thus: "Through one man sin entered the world, and death through sin, and thus death spread to all men, because all sinned" (Rom. 5:12; cf. Rom. 6:23; 1 Cor. 15:22). Death is not natural but "foreign and hostile to human life; it is an expression of divine anger (Ps. 90:7, 11), a judgment (Rom. 1:32), a condemnation (Rom. 5:16), and a curse (Gal. 3:13), and fills the hearts of the children of men with dread and fear, just because it is felt to be something unnatural."[4]

In addition to physical death, sin's curse brings moral death—a deterioration of the experience of divine image-bearing. Where the curse reigns, humans are dead in trespasses and sins (Eph. 2:1). If uncured, sin's curse leads to eternal death. This grim reality helps us treasure the promise of the gospel: all who live by faith in God's Son are redeemed from the law's curse, since Christ has become a curse for them (Gal. 3:10–13). Understanding the cause of death is vitally important. If death is natural, then we must simply accept it. But if death is caused by sin, and if sin is defeated, then death can be reversed (2 Tim. 1:10). As Jesus told Martha, while both of them grieved the death of their friend and brother Lazarus, it is possible to taste death and not thoroughly die (John 11:23–27).

Preparing for Death

For each of us, death is both imminent and unpredictable. Every week the local paper contains obituaries of both old and young people. Some expected to die; others were blindsided. No one

---

3. On covenant headship and original sin see, for example, John Calvin, *Institutes of the Christian Religion* (Grand Rapids: Eerdmans, 1962), 2.1.; John Murray, *The Imputation of Adam's Sin* (Phillipsburg, N.J.: Presbyterian and Reformed, 1959); and Michael Grant Brown and Zach Keele, *Sacred Bond: Covenant Theology Explored*, 2nd ed. (Grand Rapids: Reformed Fellowship, 2017), 47–48.

4. Berkhof, *Systematic Theology*, 669.

can cheat death. But we can prepare for death so that our deaths will not be eternal punishment for our sin, "but only a dying to sin and an entering into eternal life" (John 5:24; Rom. 7:24–25; Phil. 1:23).[5]

In Charlotte Bronte's *Jane Eyre*, young Jane is asked if she knows where bad children go when they die.

> "They go to hell" was my ready and orthodox answer.
> "And what is hell? Can you tell me that?"
> "A pit full of fire."
> "And should you like to fall into that pit and to be burning there forever?"
> "No sir."
> "What must you do to avoid it?"
> I deliberated a moment. My answer when it did come was objectionable. "I must keep in good health and not die."[6]

How many people are like Jane, trying to prevent death rather than prepare for the life to come with true godliness (see 1 Tim. 4:8)?[7]

Prepare for Death by Entrusting Yourself to Christ

No one is ready to die who is not entrusting their eternity to the eternal Son of God. The only way to die well is to become "hidden with Christ in God" (Col. 3:3) so that Christ's life, death, and resurrection become yours. In His death Christ has borne for us the wrath of God against our sin (Heb. 2:9).[8] He was raised to "overcome death…make us partakers of the righteousness which He has obtained for us by his death," raise us up to a new life, and

---

5. Heidelberg Catechism (henceforth HC) 42.

6. Charlotte Bronte, *Jane Eyre* (New York: Century Co., 1906), 30

7. For more on answering this vital question, see Joel R. Beeke and Christopher W. Bogosh, *Death and Dying: Getting Rightly Prepared for the Inevitable* (Grand Rapids: Reformation Heritage Books, 2018).

8. HC 40.

offer a "sure pledge of our blessed resurrection."[9] God graciously offers us the eternal life we forfeited by our union with Adam (original sin), and by our actual transgressions.[10] We can receive God's gift "and make it [our] own in no other way than by faith only" (1 John 5:10).[11]

Prepare for Death by Bearing Fruit

Economists—armed with striking compound-interest graphs—tirelessly urge us to start investing early for the golden years. Still, too many people enter old age woefully, financially unprepared. Similarly, too few people value Jesus's admonition to "lay up for yourselves treasures in heaven" (Matt. 6:20). John Piper reflects on Jesus's words:

> Evidently there are two ways to live: you can live with a view to accumulating valuable things on earth, or you can live with a view to accumulating valuable things in heaven. Jesus says: the mark of a Christian is that his eyes are on heaven and he measures all his behavior by what effect it will have on heaven—everlasting joy with God.[12]

Those who commit to investing in eternity—by beginning as soon as possible, working hard, and finishing well—by God's grace, store up treasure in heaven.

Prepare for Death by Meditating on Death

Macabre meditation can be unhealthy. But it doesn't have to be.[13] As evidence, and as a pattern for our reflection, Scripture

---

9. HC 45.

10. See Westminster Shorter Catechism 18.

11. HC 61.

12. John Piper, "Don't Be Anxious, Lay up Treasure in Heaven, Part 1," *Desiring God* (blog), March 2, 2003, http://www.desiringgod.org/messages/dont-be-anxious-lay-up-treasure-in-heaven-part-1.

13. See, for example, Abraham Kuyper, *In the Shadow of Death: Meditations for the Sick-room and at the Death-bed* (Audubon, N.J.: Old Paths Publications, 1994);

frequently speaks of death. The words *death*, *dead*, and *die* occur more often than *life*, *alive*, and *live*, recorded more than one thousand times. God laments over His people's lack of thought on ultimate things: "Oh, that they were wise, that they understood this, that they would consider their latter end!" (Deut. 32:29). Moses understood and asked God to "teach us to number our days, that we may gain a heart of wisdom" (Ps. 90:12). The psalmist's currently out-of-style yearning to thoughtfully engage his own death is compelling evidence of Scripture's timeless relevance.

> Make me, O Lord, to know my end,
> Teach me the measure of my days,
> That I may know how frail I am
> And turn from pride and sinful ways.[14]

Likewise, Christian hymns teach us to find in Christ's presence hope for life and death. The death-conscious believer prays that God would "hold Thou Thy cross before my closing eyes."[15]

Hymns can help us trust God to shepherd us even though He leads us to death:

> And when at last my race is run,
> The Savior's work in me is done,
> E'en death's cold wave I will not flee,
> Since God through Jordan leadeth me.[16]

They help us process the inevitable—one day we will all long to be reclothed with immortality:

> When in dust and ashes to the grave I sink,
> When heav'n's glory flashes o'er the shelving brink,

---

and John Donne, *Devotions upon Emergent Occasions* and *Death's Duel* (New York: Random House, 1999).

14. Metrical version of Psalm 39 from *The Psalter* (Grand Rapids: Reformation Heritage Books, 1999), 104.

15. *Trinity Psalter Hymnal*, 159.

16. *Trinity Psalter Hymnal*, 600.

On thy truth relying through that mortal strife,
Lord, receive me, dying, to eternal life.[17]

Modern reluctance to think, talk, and sing about death could signify a superstitious attitude about, an unpreparedness for, and an unhealthy fear of death.[18] Christians, for whom Christ has sanctified the grave, should not be overwhelmed by fear of death.

But we most certainly should grieve death.

Grieving Death

Believers lament death because it testifies to Satan's treason and man's fallen nature. More concretely we grieve because a very real part of the deceased person's life is over. We miss them. We are saddened over the destruction of their "earthly house, this tent," their body (2 Cor. 5:1). The contemporary custom of labeling funerals as "celebrations of life," while well-intentioned, threatens to underestimate the tragedy of death. Our celebrations of the life of departed loved ones should never paint over the genuine distress (2 Sam. 1:26) we feel over the departure of our friends. Jesus wept (John 11:35). These two words express a world of wonder: God cried. Indeed, "He groaned in the spirit and was troubled" (v. 33). In full understanding that Lazarus was not lost, Jesus grieved over the treachery of the curse and in protest over the stinking corpse of a man who had previously been strong, beautiful, and good, made in the image of God. Believers must feel the freedom to cry, trusting that God puts our tears into His bottle and records them in His book (Ps. 56:8).

At the same time, believers must resist grieving inordinately, sorrowing as others who have no hope (1 Thess. 4:13).[19] Extreme

---

17. *Trinity Hymnal* (Suwanee, Ga.: Great Commission Publications, 1990), 568.

18. Pastoral experience indicates that even in the church, God's people seldom feel the freedom to say with Jacob (Gen. 48:21) or Joseph (50:24), "I am dying." One can't help but notice how our reluctance robs us of the beautifully frank conversations our forebears had with their loved ones on the brink of death.

19. See also Second Helvetic Confession 26.2.

efforts to remember departed loved ones can unintentionally conflict with God's plan for our healing. Perhaps this is why God told His people, "You shall not make any cuttings in your flesh for the dead, nor tattoo any marks on you: I am the LORD" (Lev. 19:28). Not only is the practice heathen in origin, but it tends to artificially extend the grieving process and falsely suggest that self-imposed pain is redemptive.

By contrast, David engaged the crushing blow of the death of a child in a way that respected God's gift of healing. Though filled with sadness, "David arose from the ground, washed and anointed himself, and changed his clothes; and he went into the house of the LORD and worshiped. Then he went to his own house; and when he requested, they set food before him, and he ate" (2 Sam. 12:20). David understood that he could not bring back his son from the dead and should make no attempt to do so, even symbolically. He measured his grief against God's prom- ise to be a God to him and his son (Gen. 17:7). He modeled the believer's perspective of hope, insisting that he would one day see his son on the day of resurrection (2 Sam. 12:23).

But how do we grieve for departed unbelievers? In these moments of seemingly unredeemable tragedy we need to reserve judgment to God. We should be careful of declaring the eternal fate of the dead by condemning them to hell or by marshaling false comfort of their salvation. When faced with terrible ques- tions about God's judgment against sinners, we should content ourselves with the posture of Abraham: "Shall not the Judge of all the earth do right?" (Gen. 18:25).

Honoring the Dead

Part of the typical grieving process involves a funeral or memorial service. How should we use funerals to help cultivate an end- times spirituality?

Attend the Funeral

Part of our reasonable service to our merciful God is to "weep with those who weep" (Rom. 12:15). When funerals impose on our schedules—even the funerals of lesser-known acquaintances—our attendance helps comfort the grieving. The funeral is not, after all, for the deceased but for the living, including ourselves. There is often no medicine for the soul like a gospel-infused memorial service if we follow John Donne's advice. "By this consideration of another's danger I take mine own into contemplation, and so secure myself, by making recourse to my God, who is our only security."[20]

Don't Say Too Much

In an increasingly secular world, funerals represent rapidly shrinking sacred ground. Few settings better remind us that "God is in heaven, and you on earth; therefore let your words be few" (Eccl. 5:2). Silence is a modern taboo. But in the valley of the shadow of death it can be a healing balm. When Job's friends heard that all his children had tragically died under the weight of a collapsed house, "each one came from his own place...sat down with him on the ground seven days and seven nights, and no one spoke a word to him, for they saw that his grief was very great" (Job 2:11, 13). But they grew impatient of silence. Their mouths began to pour out counsel, prompting Job to answer, "I have heard many such things; miserable counselors are you all! Shall words of wind have an end?" (Job 16:2–3). If we are anxious about what to say to the bereaved, we should remember that "I'm so sorry for your loss" will usually suffice. Those in the clutches of grief are not looking for logic but comfort. At all costs, avoid trite phrases like, "This will work out for your good" or "Isn't God great?"

---

20. John Donne, *Devotions*, 103–4.

Insist on God-Centered Funerals
Very often, bereaved families are able to heavily influence the memorial service of their loved one.[21] This means that family members can and should give careful thought to how the funeral will best honor God. A basic guideline is to not make the deceased the focal point. Over a century ago, Abraham Kuyper observed, "Sometimes in so offensive a way you hear addresses at the grave, when he, whose breath was in his nostrils, and now died, is exalted as in a halo of glory, and every remembrance of the name of the Lord remains wanting."[22] It is perfectly appropriate for the family to ask of the funeral officiant that "a brief homily should be given after the gospel, but without any kind of funeral eulogy."[23] Funerals should be both biblical and personal. But eulogies tend to crowd out the preaching time, provide ample opportunity to communicate bad theology, and exaggerate the deceased's good qualities, minimizing their need for God's grace. Might it not be best, if a eulogy seems necessary, to leave it for the fellowship time following the funeral, not unlike what often happens at weddings? If a eulogy must be given, it should be brief, true, simple, and God-centered.

Honor the Body
The witness of Scripture is unambiguous: human bodies are made by God, bear His image, can be indwelt and sanctified by the Holy Spirit, and should therefore be treated with respect after death. The burials of Sarah, Abraham, Isaac, Jacob, Lazarus, and Jesus illustrate how God's people have always cared for the bodies

---

21. The position of the United Reformed Churches in North America is helpful advice: "A Christian funeral is neither a service of corporate worship nor subject to ecclesiastical government, but is a family matter, and should be conducted accordingly." *Church Order of the United Reformed Churches in North America*, 8th ed., article 49.

22. Kuyper, *In the Shadow of Death*, 299.

23. From *Ordo Exsequiarum*, no. 41, cited in John Allyn Melloh, "Homily or Eulogy? The Dilemma of Funeral Preaching," *Worship* 67 (November 1993): 502.

of the departed.[24] The Bible's few examples of cremation (Josh. 7:25; 1 Sam. 31:12; 1 Kings 13:1–3; and Amos 2:1, for example) illustrate God's displeasure toward the deceased. There is no question: "God's method was burial, not cremation."[25] Following the tradition of the Old Testament believers, Christians from the time of the apostles until the late twentieth century almost uniformly buried their dead. The first cremation in America didn't happen until 1876. It was "accompanied by readings from Charles Darwin and the Hindu Scriptures."[26] No Christian should doubt that God is able to resurrect bodies whether they were buried or cremated, but, despite social and financial pressure to favor cremation, a Christian burial seems to best reflect a robust hope in a bodily resurrection. With planning and creativity, a God-honoring funeral can cost much less than the North American average of seven to ten thousand dollars.[27]

How we face death should be understood as the premier test of our life. After all, "when a person dies, we can see much more clearly who they really turned out to be, which is eternally significant…. When a season of life ends, we see, at least to some degree, the true fruit of all our dreaming, planning, labor and investment."[28] What Isaiah said to Hezekiah, God says to all of us: "Set your house in order, for you shall die and not live" (Isa. 38:1). With a biblical vision for the future and held tightly in the hand of God, these jarring words can also be words of hope.

---

24. See Gen. 23:19; 25:9–10; 35:29; 50:13; John 11; 19:38–42.

25. Loraine Boettner, *Immortality* (Philadelphia: Presbyterian and Reformed, 1956), 52.

26. Timothy George, "Cremation Confusion: Is it Unscriptural for a Christian to be Cremated?," *Christianity Today*, May 2002: 66.

27. See, for example, Kaitlyn Wells, "Seven Ways to Save on Funeral Costs," *Market Watch*, March 30, 2014, http://www.marketwatch.com/story/7-ways-to-save-on-funeral-costs-2014-03-27.

28. John Bloom, "Lord, Prepare Me to End Well," *Desiring God* (blog), February 28, 2017, http://www.desiringgod.org/articles/lord-prepare-me-to-end-well.

CHAPTER 4

Between Death and the End

A poet, writing about the death of a fellow man, observed this: "His soul is gone, whither? Who saw it come in, or who saw it go out? Nobody; yet everybody is sure he had one, and hath none."[1]

When a person dies, it is clear to everyone that a vital aspect of the deceased's life has ended. But is it possible for a life to truly be over at death? Can one's spirit simply terminate? Or, does it live on? In Job's words, "If a man dies, shall he live again?" (Job 14:14). On many other themes, natural theology can be tested against experience. But when it comes to life after death, without revelation we could only answer our questions with unsatisfying, inconsistent guesses.[2]

The Bible gives us answers—not the kind of answers meant to indulge all our curiosities, but answers sufficient to warn against living aimlessly and adopting the shortsighted worldview of the materialist: "Let us eat and drink, for tomorrow we die!" (1 Cor. 15:32). Scripture testifies that at death "the dust" of our bodies "will return to the earth" from which they came, "and the spirit[s]

---

1. John Donne, *Devotions upon Emergent Occasions and Death's Duel* (New York: Random House, 1999), 108.

2. Therefore, as I observed recently while on vacation, the same front page of a newspaper can contain quotes about how the recently deceased Mary Tyler Moore will live forever through her film legacy, as well as the chart numbers for Taylor Swift's "I Don't Wanna Live Forever."

will return to God who gave" them (Eccl. 12:7). Beyond this, what can we say about life after death and before the return of Christ?

Death Cannot Destroy Souls

Not surprisingly, many people—even those without a biblical worldview—expect life after death. Almost no one can look at a dead body and conclude that the person's life has been completely extinguished. People often sense that life, which is so real, so precious, and interconnected, cannot simply cease when the body fails. Even those who reject a literal notion of life after death still insist on the never-dying remembrance of the deceased, a hollow comfort given the brevity of our individual and corporate memories (Eccl. 1:11). This very expectation of life after death seems to be a testimony to the continued existence of the soul. Herman Bavinck wrote, "In the case of the belief of the immortality of the soul…we are dealing…with a conviction that was not gained by reflection and reasoning but precedes all reflection and springs spontaneously from human nature as such. It is self-evident and natural, and is found wherever no philosophical doubts have undermined it." In Solomon's words, God "has put eternity in [our] hearts" (Eccl. 3:11). We sense eternity. We yearn for it. Our lives are terribly abridged without it. Bavinck put it this way: "The so-called arguments for immortality…are witnesses *of*, not grounds *for*, the belief in immortality…. The rational, moral, consciousness of humans points to a psychic existence that reaches beyond the visible world. That which by virtue of its nature seeks the eternal must be destined for eternity."[3]

The Bible confirms that the soul will outlive the body of the dead, as illustrated in Jesus's parable of the rich man and Lazarus (Luke 16:19–31). Jesus says that the death of the body does not kill the soul, and the value of a human is not spent simply

---

3. Herman Bavinck, *The Last Things: Hope for This World and the Next* (Grand Rapids: Baker, 1996), 25, 27.

because their body decays (Matt. 10:28–31). A person's soul does not depend on this body; it was Adam's soul, his spirit, that made him a living being (1 Cor. 15:45).

You have a never-dying soul. A person might mistreat his body (ignorantly), supposing that in a hundred years it won't make any difference.[4] But your soul will outlive your body. "For what will it profit a man if he gains the whole world, and loses his own soul? Or what will a man give in exchange for his soul?" (Mark 8:36–37).

Death Ends a Time of Decision

Dying is like casting a completed ballot into a locked box. Even before the vote is counted, the choice is irretrievable. Death seals the eternal destiny of everyone. Paul writes, "For we must all appear before the judgment seat of Christ, that each one may receive the things done in the body, according to what he has done, whether good or bad" (2 Cor. 5:10). This life in the body is a probation for the life to come. Here and now we decide whether we desire to spend eternity in God's restored kingdom, or if we would rather cast our lot with the kingdoms of this earth that will one day be put under the feet of King Jesus (1 Cor. 15:24–25). Jesus's parable of the talents ends with this dreadful judgment against the one who failed to invest in eternity: "Cast the unprofitable servant into the outer darkness. There will be weeping and gnashing of teeth" (Matt. 25:30). Our undying souls confirm our accountability to the One who has given them to us. We should "fear Him who is able to destroy both soul and body in hell" (Matt. 10:28).

Scripture mentions no postmortem opportunity for an unconverted person to be made right with God. The medieval Roman

---

4. On the importance of caring for our bodies, see David Murray, "The Most Overlooked Doctrine," *HeadHeartHand* (blog), November 1, 2012, http://head hearthand.org/blog/2012/11/01/the-most-overlooked-doctrine/.

Catholic Church developed a theory of purgatory suggesting that those who were not sufficiently prepared to go straight to God after death could be further refined by fire. But Jesus could not have been more clear: after death, the souls of the deceased are in a place either of torment or of blessedness, between the two of which a great gulf is fixed to prevent passage from one place to another (Luke 16:26). Further, "purgatory is but an extension of the doctrine of penance, which denies the sufficiency of Christ's active and passive obedience."[5]

Outside the church an even less clear notion exists that God's punishment, even the punishment of death, is always restorative. Nearly ubiquitous in our culture is the belief that those who die must go on to a better place. Sinclair Ferguson has said, "The greatest heresy of the western world is the heresy that we are acceptable to God simply because we have died." The dominant cultural assumption is that "we are justified by dying."[6] The Bible insists that immortality is only brought to light through the gospel of Christ (2 Tim. 1:10), not by the act of dying.

The writer to the Hebrews warns against wasting opportunities to believe the gospel and enter into God's rest. He very forcefully identifies the "certain day" on which you shall believe: "Today, if you will hear His voice, do not harden your hearts" (Heb. 4:7). The psalm from which the writer draws this phrase is riddled with the word *come* and other similar exhortations to meet with God and give Him the honor due Him while life persists (Ps. 95:1, 2, 6). When the day of grace is over, those who come to God will only know His wrath (v. 11). If you have not yet come to God, seeking and finding the gift of eternal life through Christ, do so today. Life sometimes offers "second chances." But at death, second chances expire without warning.

---

5. Michael Horton, *Christian Faith* (Grand Rapids: Zondervan, 2011), 913.
6. Sinclair Ferguson, *Judgment: The Final Verdict*, unpublished sermon, http://tapesfromscotland.org/Audi06/6714.mp3.

Death Unites *and* Distinguishes Believers and Unbelievers

The modern church might be surprised—even unsettled—at the historic church's position that until the second coming the dead are all united in a common state of disembodied waiting. The Bible uses the words *sheol* (in the Old Testament) and *hades* (in the New Testament) to describe the situation in which "not only the wicked but also believers find themselves...after death."[7] In Acts 2:27, for example, Peter quotes from Psalm 16:10 in which David prophesied of the Christ, that God would not leave His soul in sheol. Both righteous David and Christ, along with unrighteous Shimei (1 Kings 2:8–9, 36–46) and Korah (Num. 16:1–33), entered sheol at death. In a very general sense, sheol (and hades) captures the negative aspects of losing one's life. Sheol is not so much a place as the state of death, the experience of the separation of body and soul.[8] Sheol is like a city that exists outside the land of the living (Ps. 52:5; Prov. 15:24), a city barred by massive gates (Matt. 16:18; Rev. 1:18) through which no one can escape by their own power.[9] All the dead in sheol—both the righteous

---

7. Bavinck, *Last Things*, 36. Both words have diverse meanings and are not exactly synonyms. They are often, though improperly, translated as "hell" in English translations (see Acts 2:27 KJV). See also Louis Berkhof, *Systematic Theology* (Grand Rapids: Eerdmans, 1939), 686.

8. Bavinck, *Last Things*, 685.

9. On the possibility of one returning from sheol to the land of the living, the Second Helvetic Confession (art. 26) is instructive:

Now that which is recorded of the spirits or souls of the dead sometimes appearing to them that are alive, and craving certain duties of them whereby they may be set free: we count those apparitions among the delusions, crafts, and deceits of the devil, who, as he can transform himself into an angel of light so he labors tooth and nail either to overthrow the true faith or else to call it into doubt. The Lord, in the Old Testament, forbade to enquire the truth of the dead and to have anything to do with spirits (Deut. 18:10–11). And to the glutton, being bound in torments, as the truth of the gospel declares, is denied any return to his brethren; the oracles of God pronouncing and saying, "They have Moses and the prophets, let them hear them. If they hear not Moses and the prophets, neither will they believe, if one shall arise from the dead" (Luke 16:29, 31).

and the wicked—have lost the gift of a rich, uniquely earthly life and have received the wages of sin (Rom. 6:23). The dead experience a certain "diminution of life, a deprivation of everything in this life that makes for its enjoyment."[10] In this sense, while for believers death is "not a satisfaction for our sins,"[11] it is "the culmination of the chastisements which God has ordained for the sanctification of his people."[12]

The dead enter a common state from which they can only leave when death and hades deliver up their dead at the day of resurrection (Rev. 20:13). Still, in this intermediate state, the believing and unbelieving dead are greatly distinguished.

Unbelievers in the Intermediate State

Even before they die, because of their persistent unbelief, unbelievers are condemned already (John 3:18, 36). At death condemned, unbelieving spirits are locked in prison (1 Peter 3:19) from which they await the final judgment. While not yet cast into the lake of fire (Rev. 20:15) those who have died apart from Christ begin at death a time of torment. So, the rich man in Jesus's parable was not tormented because he was in the place of the dead, but because for him, the place of the dead was the narthex of hell (Luke 16:23). To die as an unbeliever is to lose the best of this life and to enter a worse state, while awaiting even worse things to come.

Believers in the Intermediate State

For those who die in the Lord (Rev. 14:13), the intermediate state is a loss of that which is precious in the present life. But this loss is so outweighed by the glory of the life to come that death can be called great gain (Phil. 1:21). The apostle Paul—persecuted in flesh (2 Cor. 11:22–29), frustrated by his sin (Rom. 7:13–25), and

---

10. Bavinck, *Last Things*, 31.
11. HC 42.
12. See Berkhof, *Systematic Theology*, 670.

having already tasted paradise (2 Cor. 12:1–6)—had no doubt: to depart from this life and be with Christ is far better (Phil. 1:23).[13] All believers can be "confident, yes, well pleased rather to be absent from the body and to be present with the Lord" (2 Cor. 5:8). All who trust in Christ can take His promise as their last earthly thought: "Assuredly, I say to you, today you will be with Me in Paradise" (Luke 23:43). At this very moment, there is a "church of the firstborn who are registered in heaven" made up of "the spirits of just men made perfect" (Heb. 12:23). The dead in Christ begin to rest from their labors and enjoy the fruit of their works (Heb. 4:9–10; Rev. 6:11; 14:13).

Because of these texts, a believer can say, "My soul after this life shall be immediately taken up to Christ its head."[14] As summed up by writers in the sixteenth and seventeenth centuries, "We believe that the faithful, after bodily death, go directly unto Christ,"[15] for their souls are then "made perfect in holiness" and are "received into the highest heavens."[16]

Death Begins a Time of Anticipation

Every grain in the hourglass of time is eagerly making way for the coming of Christ, the resurrection of the body, the final judgment, and the breaking in of the age to come. Even those in the intermediate state have not arrived; they do not know the full coming of the future age.

The wicked dead anticipate the judgment with unrelenting dread. Those who live in unbelief can often chase off thoughts of judgment. But those who have died in unbelief cannot escape

---

13. With Paul's desire to depart the flesh and be with the Lord, "Any idea of an unconscious state following death or of a purgatorial discipline in the next world is denied by the sheer simplicity of Paul's expectation." Ralph Martin, *The Epistle of Paul to the Philippians: An Introduction and Commentary*, Tyndale New Testament Commentaries (Grand Rapids: Eerdmans, 1999), 81–82.

14. HC 57.

15. Second Helvetic Confession, art. 26.

16. WLC 86.

"a certain fearful expectation of judgment, and fiery indignation which will devour the adversaries" (Heb. 10:27). When
the deceased unbeliever realizes he has lost his opportunity for
repentance and awaits dreadful judgment, he can only cry "to the
mountains and rocks, 'Fall on us and hide us from the face of
Him who sits on the throne and from the wrath of the Lamb!'"
(Rev. 6:16). For those who die without Christ as their mediator,
the prospect of torment is no longer an uncertain "if" but an ago-
nizing "when" (Matt. 8:29).

By contrast, the righteous dead anticipate the judgment with
inexhaustible delight. Prior to the resurrection of the dead, even
those who have died in Christ are not satisfied. Their souls are
perfected but they eagerly wait for the resurrection of their bodies
and the realization of their full deliverance.[17] Those who are in
heaven now await the day of judgment, crying with a loud voice,
"How long, O Lord, holy and true, until You judge and avenge
our blood on those who dwell on earth?" (Rev. 6:10). They await
the ingathering of all the saints. They await full bodily communion with their Savior. But even the anticipation of the saints in
glory does not issue from a dominating lack but a wholesome
desire to be more fully clothed (2 Cor. 5:1–5), a joyful desire to
experience God more deeply. The yearning of the blessed in paradise is a good yearning, like the way friends eagerly await the
arrival of other guests to a party.

What is so powerful about Jesus's parable of the rich man
and Lazarus is that both men, after death, could experientially
affirm the contents of this chapter. Death doesn't kill souls but it
does seal their destinies. Out of their experience, both men speak
to us. The rich man warns the living not to undervalue their
souls. Lazarus encourages God's people not to overvalue their
temporary suffering.

---

17. See BC 37.

PART THREE

GENERAL ESCHATOLOGY

CHAPTER 5

He's Coming Again

To talk about the return of Christ is to invite a torrent of questions—you know them: questions about the millennium, the timing of Christ's return, and the nature of the kingdom He will bring. These questions about Christ's return can be helpful, and we will wrestle carefully with several of them in this chapter and subsequent ones.

Because these questions are difficult to answer, they tend to lead to disagreement. Given our respective temperaments, conflict tempts us either to avoid the issue or attack our opponents. The net result is that the most significant event of human history can lose for us its crowning place in the Bible's story of redemption. To say it differently, if Christ's return is unimportant to us, or if we equate Christ's return with our theory of the millennium, for example, we are not properly reading the climactic chapter of God's story.

Recently one of our children finished a book only to discover that the last few chapters were missing. That's a tragedy! But it would be equally tragic if, in the place of the last few chapters, someone had inserted a highly condensed summary of the ending, followed by pages of technical literary analysis and point/counterpoint discussion of the story's resolution. That's sometimes how Christians reflect on the return of Christ. *What's your view of the millennium?* isn't a terrible question. But it is a terrible replacement for the wonder and awe we should experience when we reflect on how God will resolve this present age.

The return of Jesus as a historical event—the final historical event of this present age—cannot be understood apart from the rest of the history of this age. To put it briefly, this present age is a time of redemption.

The Context of Christ's Return

That the present state of things is not all right does not need to be argued; we experience this fact in myriad ways. What is more challenging is to articulate why everything is wrong. If we could retell the story of the world from the beginning until now, we would quickly realize that the two connected concepts of sin and God's presence are at the heart of that story. Only when we grasp the relationship between these two realities can we understand Christ's return.

Everything about the first two chapters of the Bible conveys that God was intimately present in the sinless world. God's Spirit moved over the canvas of the universe, forming and filling the budding world with goodness (Gen. 1:2). So close was God to the world that His word produced substance and His breath brought life (Gen. 2:7). God made humans sufficiently like Him so that they could uniquely enjoy His presence and experience His blessing (Gen. 1:26–28). When God spoke to Adam, His voice sounded friendly; everything He said was good and well received. The end of the Bible's story hints at what the beginning was like: "Behold, the dwelling place of God is with man. He will dwell with them, and they will be his people, and God himself will be with them as their God" (Rev. 21:3 ESV). History began with Father, Son, Holy Ghost, and naked Adam and Eve, completely at peace with each other.

Notably, when the first humans sinned against God they lost the pleasure of His presence. When "they heard the sound of the LORD God walking in the garden, in the cool of the day" (Gen. 3:8), Adam and Eve did not run to Him. They ran from Him, probably fearing that God was coming to kill them (Gen. 2:17).

They, "trembling[,] fled from His presence," having made themselves "wholly miserable."[1] Having rejected God's friendship, they
turned their own way (see Isa. 53:6). Ever since, humanity's most
basic problem has been alienation from God. But in that dark
moment God began to demonstrate a divine attribute that man
had not yet known: mercy. God's love toward His people never
depended on their love for Him but on His untainted goodness.
And so, even when Adam and Eve began to despise God, He
kept loving them. He pursued them in love, calling out to Adam
(Gen. 3:9) in the way a father cries out for his children who have
become lost in a forest. When God found them He demonstrated
the guilt of their sin so they might appreciate the promises He
was about to make. At the devil's instigation they had traded their
innocence for pain. Satan had driven the wedge of sin between
God and His people. God would not overlook this evil. Instead,
He would raise up an heir of Adam and Eve to destroy the devil
and his works (1 John 3:8). God meant this promise to bolster
Adam and Eve—and their believing descendants—to retain hope
in a sad, new world. Life would become hard (Gen. 3:16–19);
God would seem less accessible (Gen. 3:22–24). But He would
never be beyond man's believing grasp (Acts 17:27).

Since the first sin, people have yearned for God's presence
even when this yearning has become obscured by distractions.
And since that first promise, God has continued a work of restoration that He will complete on the day of Christ Jesus (Phil. 1:6).

The rest of the Bible provides glimpses into what the
restored presence of God will be like. God continued to retain a
remnant of people who would "call on the name of the LORD"
(Gen. 4:26), keeping alive hope that God had not altogether for-
saken His world. God later chose Abraham to be the father of
a special people who would show "all the families of the earth"
the blessedness of knowing God (Gen. 12:3). God promised His

---

1. BC 17.

people: "I will set My tabernacle among you, and My soul shall not abhor you. I will walk among you and be your God, and you shall be My people" (Lev. 26:11–12). The physical tabernacle and the later temples were physical testimonies of God's promise to be among His people.

It makes perfect sense then, that when God sent His Son—the Word become flesh, God born of a woman (Gal. 4:4)—to break the curse and open up a new and living way to God, He "dwelt among us" (John 1:14); literally, He tabernacled among us. God was again among men, preaching good news, healing up broken hearts, announcing liberty to captives, giving sight to the blind, and liberating the oppressed (Luke 4:18).

But God was not yet ready to restore all things. Christ died like a sinner (2 Cor. 5:21), was raised in an imperishable body, and "was taken up" from His disciples into heaven (Acts 1:11) to continue working redemption until the time was right to be finished. In exchange for His physical presence, Christ left the Holy Spirit as a guarantee (2 Cor. 5:5) that when our present tabernacles, our bodies, are destroyed we will "have a building from God, a house not made with hands, eternal in the heavens" (2 Cor. 5:1). The Spirit is God's guarantee that He will keep His promise (2 Cor. 1:22) to again live with us in unrestricted freedom. The Spirit guarantees that God's people will not miss out on their inheritance, which is not a legacy of possessions but a bequest of belonging, God's prized possession will be bought back from a foreign land by the blood of Christ (Eph. 1:14).

In the light of the whole history of redemption Peter preaches the return of Christ.

Repent therefore and be converted, that your sins may be blotted out, so that times of refreshing may come from the presence of the Lord, and that He may send Jesus Christ, who was preached to you before, whom heaven must receive until the times of restoration of all things, which God has spoken by the mouth of all His holy prophets since the world began. (Acts 3:19–21)

"Christ," says Calvin, "hath already restored all things by his death; but the effect doth not yet fully appear."[2] The barriers between God and man have not yet been completely removed. But when Christ returns He will restore full fellowship between God and His people. Toward that end Christ presently works from heaven restoring spiritual fellowship and preparing a dwelling place for the restored family of God (John 14:1–4).

Set within salvation history, it should be plain that the return of the King is not a postscript to the story of this age; it is the main event toward which this entire age leans. Neither is it a theory to debate. It is a reality that should steel our hope in God's reconciling work.

The Characteristics of Christ's Return

Within this overarching framework of God's work of restoration, several notable characteristics of Christ's return emerge.

A Literal Event

Any attempt to allegorize Jesus's promise to return to His people conflicts with the clear words of Scripture. The gospel writer Luke, writing as a historian who had "perfect understanding of all things from the very first" (Luke 1:3), pictures the apostles "gazing up into heaven" (Acts 1:11) after Jesus had just been "taken up, and a cloud received Him out of their sight" (v. 9). The two heavenly messengers told them, "This same Jesus, who was taken up from you into heaven, will so come in like manner as you saw Him go into heaven" (v. 11). As physically as Christ had been with the disciples, and was with them no more, so would He return again.

---

2. John Calvin, *Commentary upon the Acts of the Apostles*, ed. Henry Beveridge (Grand Rapids: Baker, 1989), 1:153.

At the opening of both his gospel and his first epistle, John insists that Jesus, during His incarnation, was literally, physically with His people so that He was seen with eyes, looked upon (1 John 1:1–3), and beheld (John 1:14). John likewise expected a literal, physical return of Jesus: "Behold, He is coming with clouds, and every eye will see Him, even they who pierced Him" (Rev. 1:7).

Christ's return in Scripture is not a metaphor for a revival of spirituality or the advance of Jesus's kingdom principles; a shouting, trumpeting Christ, riding the clouds (1 Thess. 4:16) is an unsuitable metaphor for a mere symbolic return. The hope of the gospel is not a restored sense of closeness with God but the actual "presence of our Lord Jesus Christ at His coming" (1 Thess. 2:19). Faith desires to lay hold not merely of Jesus's ideals, but of Jesus Himself. The only satisfying and comforting vision of the end is to "always be with the Lord" (1 Thess. 4:17). Only Christ's literal second coming is salvation (Heb. 9:28).

A Certain Event

Because of its central place in God's plan of restoration it is no wonder that Christ's return is an event resolutely and repeatedly promised by God. Three times in the Bible's final chapter Jesus promises, "I am coming quickly" (Rev. 22:7, 12, 20). Jesus bolstered the faith of His troubled disciples with this promise: "And if I go and prepare a place for you, I will come again and receive you to Myself; that where I am, there you may be also" (John 14:3). Not surprisingly, as the darkness of the shadow of death deepened, Jesus increasingly vowed to return after His departure (cf. Matt. 24:30; 25:31; 26:64).

But even before Jesus's first advent, God had promised to come back to His people. The New Testament reiterates a theme promoted by the prophets (Isa. 13:6; 1 Thess. 5:2; and 2 Peter 3:10, for example): the day of the Lord will be a calamitous event for the nations *particularly* because the God whom they assumed to be afar off—never to return—will come near to avenge His people and His name (see Psalm 10, esp. vv. 11–12).

God has promised to return to save His people and judge His enemies. But He tells no one the day or the hour (Matt. 24:36). Some assume that by God's delay in keeping His promise to return He is "slack concerning His promise" (2 Peter 3:9). They forget that God always keeps His promises, though they are sometimes a long time coming. They forget that "with the Lord one day is as a thousand years, and a thousand years as one day" (v. 8). C. S. Lewis writes, "As nothing outlasts God, so nothing slips away from Him into a past."[3] God is astonishingly patient. He is content to allow more time for the church to fulfill the Great Commission and for the unreached to repent.[4]

A Calculated Event

While it is not for us to "know times or seasons which the Father has put in His own authority" (Acts 1:7), Scripture does speak of signs of Christ's coming. These signs have always been evident during the last days, the time between Christ's two appearances. But they will culminate in unmistakable tokens of Christ's return immediately prior to the great day. In this way the signs of the end affirm that "the coming of our Lord is approaching" and encourage us to "be ready at any time to receive him."[5]

First, before Christ returns, "the gospel must first be preached to all the nations" (Mark 13:10; see also Matt. 24:14) to the extent that the good news becomes "a sign that calls for decision."[6] Immediately before His departure Jesus charged the church to

---

3. C. S. Lewis, *Reflections on the Psalms* (Glasgow: Fontana Books, 1958), 114.

4. So, says Calvin, "this is the reason why Christ doth not appear by and by, because the warfare of the Church is not yet full." *Commentary*, 1:153.

5. William Hendriksen, *The Bible on the Life Hereafter* (Grand Rapids: Baker, 1959), 113.

6. Berkhof, *Systematic Theology*, 698.

bring His story to the world[7] so that salvation might come to "every tribe and tongue and people and nation" (Rev. 5:9).

Second, through worldwide evangelization, the fullness of Israel will be saved. While God began His work of grace primarily among the Jewish people, "they have not all obeyed the gospel" (Rom. 10:16). With a heart overflowing with love toward his fellow Jews (Rom. 10:1), Paul uses Isaiah 65:2 to express his disappointment over Israel's general unwillingness to believe in Jesus: they are "a disobedient and contrary people" (v. 21). Still, insists Paul, "God has not cast away His people whom He foreknew" (11:2). Before Christ's return God will "turn away ungodliness" from His first people, "and so all Israel will be saved" (v. 26). Despite differing interpretations, it seems that Paul firmly hoped for a large-scale conversion of the Jewish people before the return of Christ.[8]

Third, near the end of this age, God's restraint of the devil will relax, resulting in the great apostasy and tribulation. John saw that at the end of this age, "Satan will be released from his prison and will go out to deceive the nations," making war against God's people (Rev. 20:7–8). Not only Jesus (Matt. 24:9–12, 21–24; Mark 13:9–22) but also Paul (2 Thess. 2:3; 2 Tim. 3:1–5) and John (Rev. 6:9; 7:13–14) expected God's people, especially near the end, to enter the kingdom of God through great tribulation (see Acts 14:22).

Fourth, before the true Christ returns from heaven, the spirit of antichrist, who has always been in the world (1 John 2:18; 4:3), will be manifested in a single person. During the unprecedented tribulation (Mark 13:19), "False christs and false prophets will rise and show signs and wonders to deceive, if possible, even the

---

7. See Matt. 28:18–20; Mark 16:15–16; Luke 24:46–49; Acts 1:8.

8. For a brief elaboration on this thesis, see Cornel Venema, *Christ and the Future: The Bible's Teaching about the Last Things* (Edinburgh: Banner of Truth, 2008), 59–65; and William Boekestein, "All Israel Will Be Saved: Evaluating Paul's Hope for the Jewish People," *Puritan Reformed Journal* 10, no. 2 (July 2018): 31–44.

elect" (v. 22). A single "man of sin…the son of perdition" will be "revealed" as an imposter; him "the Lord will consume with the breath of His mouth and destroy with the brightness of His coming" (2 Thess. 2:3, 8).

A Relevant Event

Christ's return is relevant exactly because it will be powerful and glorious (Mark 13:24–27). *Power* and *glory* are biblical shorthand for what makes God so unlike His creation; the terms contrast the weakness (Rom. 6:19) and vanity (see Ecclesiastes) of human life. At Christ's coming believers will trade dishonor and deficiency for glory and power (1 Cor. 15:43). A reunion with the all-glorious and almighty God (Rev. 19:1) is good news for inherently insufficient people.

Because of Christ's promise to return, we can face the disappointments of life with sure hope that God is fixing the mess we made; He has not given up on His people. We can wait for Him (1 Thess. 1:10) patiently, trusting that He is neither impulsive nor sluggish. "Therefore, we expect that great day with a most ardent desire, to the end that we may fully enjoy the promises of God in Christ Jesus our Lord."[9]

---

9. BC 37.

CHAPTER 6

A Thousand Years?

Much of the end-times disagreement among believers stems from differing interpretations of the millennium of Revelation 20. Regrettably, debate over the millennium is often the sum of what Christians understand to be the end times. As suggested previously, our view of the millennium is not our eschatology but merely an aspect of it. Our apprehension of the last things should be much richer and broader than how we understand the relationship of Christ's return to this thousand years. The especially American preoccupation with the millennium suggests a theological imbalance.[1]

Still, the millennium of Revelation 20, whatever it means, invites our study. In this chapter, six times the phrase "thousand years" is used to describe a period of time in which Satan is bound and therefore unable to deceive the nations (vv. 2–3, 7), in which martyred witnesses and priests of God live and reign with Christ (vv. 4, 6), and in which some of the dead still anticipate a resurrection (v. 5). How do these verses help us understand and yearn for the return of Jesus?

---

1. The mere title of Charles Ryrie's *The Basis of the Premillennial Faith* is anecdotal evidence of how a theory of Christ's return can inappropriately be elevated to the essence of the Christian faith.

The Leading Positions

The respective positions on the millennium each answer these questions: What are the "thousand years," and when do they occur, especially in relation to Jesus's return?

Premillennialism

Premillennialists believe the millennium to be a literal thousand year period in which Christ will reign on earth after His return.

Historic premillennialism[2] can be summarized as follows. Prior to Christ's second coming, the spiritual conditions of this present age will steadily decline, especially near the end. The Antichrist will subject the church to great persecution. At the appointed time Christ will return from heaven, destroy Antichrist and his allies, physically resurrect the saints and convert the Jewish people—restoring them to their land[3]—and inaugurate a thousand-year kingdom of God on earth in which righteousness will flourish. At the end of the millennium God will, for a second time, raise the dead and judge everyone who has lived. He will then create a new heaven and earth in which He will dwell forever with His people, having confined to hell the devil, the rest of the fallen angels, and all unbelievers.

---

2. See George Eldon Ladd, *The Presence of the Future: The Eschatology of Biblical Realism* (Grand Rapids: Eerdmans, 1974).

3. Thanks to John Jeffery for pointing out to me that the physical restoration of land to the Jewish people is not universally held among historic premillennialists, some of whom are supersessionists (what has also been labeled "replacement theology"). George Eldon Ladd is an influential example of a historical premillennialist who would deny such future fulfillments to national Israel. See Barry Horner, *Future Israel: Why Christian Anti-Judaism Must Be Challenged*, in the *New American Commentary Studies in Bible and Theology*, series ed. E. Ray Clendenen (Nashville: B&H Academic, 2007), 180–83, s.v. "The Hermeneutic of George Eldon Ladd." Citations from Ladd's writings include George Eldon Ladd, "Historic Premillennialism," in *The Meaning of the Millennium: Four Views*, ed. Robert G. Clouse (Downers Grove, Ill.: InterVarsity, 1977), 23; *A Theology of the New Testament* (Grand Rapids: Eerdmans, 1993), 433; and *The Last Things* (Grand Rapids: Eerdmans, 1978), 9–18.

Starting in the early nineteenth century, premillennialism became influenced by the hermeneutic of dispensationalism.[4] In this theology, redemptive history is generally divided into seven periods of testing called dispensations.[5] At the end of the dispensation of law (from Moses to Christ), God sent His Son to restore His kingdom to Israel. But, because His people rejected Christ, God suspended His unique dealings with Israel and began a completely separate and temporary church age. When this "dispensation of grace" ends, God will finally establish the kingdom with Israel during the final dispensation, the millennial age. According to this view, Christ will usher in the millennium in this way: first He will return in the clouds to raise deceased believers and rapture living believers to Himself. While the church is with the Lord, out of the world, the Jewish people will finally embrace the message of the kingdom; those who believe will endure a terrible persecution. At the end of seven years Christ will come to earth with the church,[6] bind Satan for a thousand years, and fulfill

---

4. See Charles Ryrie, *Dispensationalism* (Chicago: Moody, 2007). It should be noted that despite dispensationalism's significant influence, historic premillennialism remains a prevalent contemporary eschatology. See George Eldon Ladd, *The Blessed Hope: A Biblical Study of the Second Advent and the Rapture* (Grand Rapids: Eerdmans, 1956).

5. On the differing number of dispensations identified among dispensationalists see, for example, Charles Caldwell Ryrie, *Dispensationalism*, rev. ed. (Chicago: Moody, 2007, 1995; 1966 as *Dispensationalism Today*), 51–54. "Occasionally a dispensationalist may hold as few as four, and some hold as many as eight." *Dispensationalism*, 53.

6. It might be noted (again, with thanks to John Jeffery) that, especially among some of the older traditional dispensationalists, the church is not seen as returning "to earth" with Christ. Clarence Larkin is one who is usually understood as depicting the church as above the earth during the millennium. On this teaching see J. Dwight Pentecost, *Things to Come: A Study in Biblical Eschatology* (Grand Rapids: Zondervan, 1958), 577–79. John Walvoord presents this teaching as follows:

> If the new Jerusalem is in existence throughout the millennial reign of Christ, it is possible that it is a satellite city suspended over the earth during the thousand-year reign of Christ as the dwelling place of resurrected and translated saints who also have access to the earthly scene. This would help

all God's promises for the Jews, including the rebuilding of the temple at Jerusalem and the restoration of sacrifices.[7]

A more contemporary movement, known as progressive dispensationalism, minimizes the traditional dispensational distinction between Israel and the church, and it recognizes that the promises made to Israel are, even in this present age, being partly fulfilled in the church.[8]

Postmillennialism

Postmillennial theologians likewise expect a more-or-less literal thousand year earthly reign of Christ, though preceding (rather than succeeding) His second coming. Postmillennialists expect "the gospel" to "in the end become immeasurably more effective than it is at present" and to "usher in a period of rich spiritual blessings for the Church of Jesus Christ, a golden age, in which the Jews will also share in the blessings of the gospel in

---

explain an otherwise difficult problem of the dwelling place of resurrected and translated beings on the earth during a period in which men are still in their natural bodies and living ordinary lives. If so, the new Jerusalem is withdrawn from the earthly scene in connection with the destruction of the old earth, and later comes down to the new earth. As presented in Revelation 21 and 22, however, the new Jerusalem is not seen as it may have existed in the past, but as it will be seen in eternity future. The possibility of Jerusalem being a satellite city over the earth during the millennium is not specifically taught in any scripture and at best is an inference based on the implication that it has been in existence prior to its introduction in Revelation 21. Its characteristics as presented here, however, are related to the eternal state rather than to the millennial kingdom.

John F. Walvoord, *The Revelation of Jesus Christ* (Chicago: Moody, 1966), 312–13, s.v. "First Vision of the New Jerusalem (21:2);" on *Bible.org*, https://bible.org/seriespage/21-new-heaven-and-new-earth [accessed March 28, 2017].

7. The restoration of blood sacrifices is generally, though not universally, held among traditional dispensationalists.

8. See Craig A. Blaising and Darrell L. Bock, *Progressive Dispensationalism* (Grand Rapids: BridgePoint, 2000). For a critical assessment of the hermeneutical foundation of this movement see Robert L. Thomas, "The Hermeneutics of Progressive Dispensationalism," *Master's Seminary Journal* 6, no. 2 (Spring 1995): 79–95.

an unprecedented manner."[9] Christ will return, according to this theory, "after the triumph of Christianity throughout the earth."[10]

Amillennialism

Contrasting both theories, amillennialism understands the thousand years of Revelation 20 as a figurative number embracing the entire age between Christ's work at Calvary and His final return in glory and power. Amillennialists "hold that the promises made to Israel…in the Old Testament are fulfilled by Jesus Christ and his church during the present age."[11] Christ is presently reigning from heaven over all history. He has bound Satan and, through His Spirit, is actively advancing the kingdom through the gospel. This position anticipates a single future return of Christ at which He will raise the dead, judge the world, and inaugurate the age to come.

Key Interpretive Principles

The widespread Christian disagreement over the millennium urges us to look beneath the respective theories and behind the contested passages to the lenses through which interpreters approach Scripture. As noted earlier, our hermeneutic—the assumptions and practices by which we interpret the Bible—precedes our interpretation.[12] Are there interpretive premises that favor an amillennial interpretation of the thousand years in Revelation 20?

---

9. Berkhof, *Systematic Theology*, 716.

10. J. Marcellus Kik, *An Eschatology of Victory* (Phillipsburg, N.J.: Presbyterian and Reformed, 1971), 4.

11. Kim Riddlebarger, *A Case for Amillennialism: Understanding the End Times* (Grand Rapids: Baker Books, 2013), 40.

12. Dispensationalist Charles Ryrie admits, "The *doctrine* of the millennial kingdom is for the dispensationalist an integral part of his entire scheme and interpretation of many Biblical passages." *Dispensationalism Today* (Chicago: Moody, 1976), 160. Emphasis added.

The Unity of the Covenants

Dispensationalists sharply distinguish Israel and the church and therefore deny that the promises made to Israel can be fulfilled in the church; the promises God made to Israel must be fulfilled to Israel. An amillennial hermeneutic acknowledges that the prophetic, projected "image of the future is Old Testament-like through and through; it is all described in terms of Israel's own history and nation. But into these sensuous earthly forms prophecy puts everlasting content."[13] When God made promises to Israel He was speaking not merely to a historical, ethnic group but to a covenant people organically connected (Rom. 11:24) to God (John 15:1–8) by faith in Christ (Heb. 4:1–2). Bavinck writes, "Therefore the New Testament is not an…interlude, neither a detour nor a departure from the line of the Old Covenant, but the long-aimed-for goal, the direct continuation and the genuine fulfillment, of the Old Testament."[14] The church made up of Jews and Gentiles (Eph. 2:11–22) can rightly inherit the promises made to Israel (Heb. 11:13–39). A covenantal understanding of Scripture eliminates an inclination to see the millennium as a unique dispensation of the kingdom of God for Israel.

The Unique Apocalyptic Genre of Revelation

As stated previously, if the book of Revelation is seen as a chronological road map of the future, and if Revelation 19 is understood to depict Christ's second coming in judgment, one will tend to read Revelation 20 through premillennial lenses.[15] But if Revelation is a multi-angled glimpse into Christ's present and future rule over all things, then the interpreter need not force each scene into a consecutive chronology.

13. Bavinck, *Last Things*, 90.
14. Bavinck, *Last Things*, 98.
15. Riddlebarger, *A Case for Amillennialism*, 223–24.

Likewise, given the symbolic character of the book,[16] "'A thousand years' is no more to be taken literally than any other number in Revelation," such as the 144,000 of Revelation 14.[17] It should be noted that outside of Revelation 20, the phrase "thousand years" is never used to describe a definite time period connected to Christ's return. In fact, in one of the other three uses of the phrase, Peter quotes Psalm 90 (v. 4) to remind believers that God does not measure a thousand years the same as we humans do (2 Peter 3:8–9).

Interpreters are bound to a basic rule that especially applies to the highly symbolic language of Revelation 20: use clear texts to interpret less clear texts.

The Biblical Tension of the Inaugurated-but-Not-Yet-Consummated Kingdom of God

When we approach Revelation 20, or similar texts, "we should not assume that biblical prophecy is weighted toward the past or the future. Rather, it is part of the 'already'/'not yet' dialectic of redemptive history."[18] The apostle John, like the prophets before him, was writing for a people who could say, "We *are* receiving a kingdom" (Heb. 12:28) even as they prayed for God's kingdom to come (Matt. 6:10). God's people have been saved (Eph. 2:8), are being saved (Acts 2:47), and will be saved through endurance (Matt. 10:22). Satan is now restrained; at the last day he will be removed. An amillennial approach can help avoid both

---

16. A helpful definition of *apocalyptic literature* will emphasize the central theme of "the coming victory of God" depicted by "means of symbolic images." McCartney and Clayton, *Let the Reader Understand*, 240. Bernard Ramm is right to say that in interpreting prophesy, including apocalyptic prophesy, "The balance in prophetic interpretation" between literalism and spiritualism "is not easy to attain." *Protestant Biblical Interpretation*, 3rd rev. ed. (Grand Rapids: Baker, 1970), 254. In fact, "in the interpretation of apocalyptic imagery a complete literalistic method is impossible." *Protestant Biblical Interpretation*, 268.

17. Joel Beeke, *Revelation*, Lectio Continua Expository Commentary on the New Testament (Grand Rapids: Reformation Heritage Books, 2016), 517.

18. Horton, *Christian Faith*, 939.

the premillennial temptation of retreatism, and the postmillennial inclination toward triumphalism. The millennium is now; the new heavens and new earth are coming.

The Thousand Years of Revelation 20:1–10

In these verses John sees current and future realities from a heavenly perspective.

Satan Is Bound (vv. 1–3)

In his vision John saw "an angel coming down from heaven, having the key to the bottomless pit and a great chain in his hand. He laid hold of the dragon, that serpent of old, who is the Devil and Satan, and bound him for a thousand years" (Rev. 20:1–2). While bound, the devil is restricted from deceiving the nations (v. 3). The dispensational assumption is that the binding of Satan is a future event reserved for the millennium.

But Jesus used strikingly similar language to describe His already-active assault on Satan's kingdom. Here is how our Lord responded to the Pharisees' accusation that He was casting out demons by the ruler of the demons: "How can one enter a strong man's house and plunder his goods, unless he first binds the strong man? And then he will plunder his house" (Matt. 12:29). Jesus, by the Spirit of God, was plundering Satan's house; this, He claimed, was a sure sign that "the kingdom of God has come upon you" (v. 28). The disciples Jesus sent out to preach the gospel perceived that the demons were subject to them in His name. Jesus agreed: "I saw Satan fall like lightning from heaven. Behold I give you authority...over all the power of the enemy" (Luke 10:17–19). Time and again the Gospels indicate that even satanic hosts understood that at Christ's coming their rule over the nations was deteriorating. Often Jesus cast out devils that had inhabited peoples of "the nations" (Matt. 8:28–34; Mark 7:26; cf. Rev. 20:3). At Pentecost the dozen nations from which 3,000 people were saved surrounded Jerusalem in every direction of the compass, stretching as far away as Rome, fifteen hundred miles west. Those who are being saved now—during the gospel age of the millennium—are a vast host from every nation, tribe, tongue, and people (Rev. 5:9).

At Christ's first coming, the dark winter of near-worldwide unbelief began turning to spring. By His death and resurrection, Jesus checked the devil's seemingly unmitigated reign of treachery. He does still prowl and devour (1 Peter 5:8), but he does so with the "desperate and angry struggle of a defeated foe."[19] Christ is loosening Satan's stranglehold on the nations. John's apocalypse is good news! And not just for those living in the millennium, but for John's original audience and for believers today. In the cross, Christ destroyed the devil (Heb. 2:14). Believers now overcome Satan "by the blood of the Lamb" shed on Calvary (Rev. 12:11). D. A. Carson writes, "The truth of the matter is that the cross marks Satan's defeat, and Satan knows it."[20] God's "victory over Satan is as decisive as if the devil were already dead and buried."[21]

The Saints Reign (vv. 4–6)

John also saw, during these thousand years, thrones upon which sat "the souls of those who had been beheaded for their witness to Jesus and for the word of God" (Rev. 20:4). Dispensationalists assert that the thousand-year reign of these souls with Christ must take place after a bodily resurrection, inaugurating Jesus's millennial reign on earth. But John seems to be communicating something different.

John does not see resurrected people but living souls. The souls of believers who had been martyred for their Christian witness had experienced a sort of resurrection, what John calls the "first resurrection." It is a resurrection reflective of Jesus's

---

19. Horton, *Christian Faith*, 942.

20. D. A. Carson, *Basics for Believers: An Exposition of Philippians* (Grand Rapids: Baker Books, 2004), 42.

21. Beeke, *Revelation*, 515.

conversation with Martha in John 11. Martha believed that one day her deceased brother Lazarus would "rise again in the resurrection at the last day" (v. 24). But Jesus corrected her. Because He is the resurrection and the life, even prior to the general resurrection, those who die in Him still live (vv. 25–26).[22] Union with Christ is a genuine resurrection. Those who are raised with Christ (Col. 3:1) will not yield to the power of the second death (Rev. 20:6). Already, prior to the general resurrection, believers are priests of God (Rev. 1:6; cf. 20:6). John, therefore, does not improperly describe the souls of martyrs in heaven as having tasted the first resurrection. By contrast "the rest of the dead"—the ungodly dead—"did not live again until the thousand years were finished" and they were raised to judgment and condemnation.[23]

To press John's vision into a literal future timetable introduces several problems. First, it overlooks the explicitly nonliteral character of the passage. How does John *see* souls? John is "showing" his readers things that cannot be seen. He is painting ideas more than literal scenes. Second, to insist that the souls in these verses have experienced the general resurrection is to minimize the importance of that resurrection as a reunion of body and soul.

Rather than describing a future millennium, John seems to be describing the blessed state of those who did not "love their lives to the death" (Rev. 12:11), who did not value their lives more than their Lord. Believers are as secure in this world as they are on the thrones of heaven. This eternal security frees us to be "faithful until death," trusting that God will give us "the crown of life" (Rev. 2:10).

---

22. So Geerhardus Vos can say, "Paul also found the principle of the resurrection in the possession of the Spirit and spoke of purely spiritual processes in terms of rising from the dead, and yet alongside of this he held to the doctrine of a literal resurrection of the body in the future." *Redemptive History,* 321.

23. Herman Hoeksema, *Behold He Cometh: An Exposition of the Book of Revelation* (Grand Rapids: Reformed Free Publishing Association, 1969), 648–49.

Satan Is Loosed and Destroyed (vv. 7–10)

John also saw the expiration of the thousand years, the end of the present age of gospel prosperity. Shortly before Jesus returns to earth, Satan will be released from his prison and will go out to deceive the nations (Rev. 20:8) "for a little while" (v. 3). For a brief season gospel progress will halt and God's people will endure unprecedented persecution. The devil will gather the deceived nations, represented as "the four corners of the earth, Gog and Magog, to gather them together to battle, whose number is as the sand of the sea" (v. 8). This great battle is a magnification of the war between the forces of good and evil which have battled since the beginning. As prophesied by Ezekiel (Ezek. 38–39), this great enemy of the church will fight against God's people but will not prevail.

God's people have never had much visible, tangible hope to see their enemies defeated. In the battle against Gog and Magog, victory for God's people seems impossible. "In these final days which shall immediately precede Christ's second coming the opposition to the church is going to be *world-wide*: the entire world, functioning as one great social and political unit under the leadership of antichristian government, will do its utmost to destroy the church."[24] All hope in a man-made age of peace, a human utopia, will expire. God's plan—as always—is to save at just the right moment, so that "the weak and helpless shall His pity know. He will surely save them from oppression's might, for their lives are precious in His holy sight."[25]

On the last day the battle will be decisively finished by the return of Christ in great power and glory. Satan does not determine how this age will end. "When antichrist's program is only half finished…when he is about to launch his final deadly attack,

---

24. William Hendriksen, *Three Lectures on the Book of Revelation* (Grand Rapids: Zondervan, 1949), 27.

25. Versification of Psalm 72:13–14 from *Psalter Hymnal* (Grand Rapids: Board of Publications of the Christian Reformed Church, 1976), 135.

then of a sudden, the heavens will open wide and our glorious Lord Jesus Christ will appear."[26] Ezekiel prophesied, "then the nations shall know that I am the LORD, the Holy One in Israel" (Ezek. 39:7).

Revelation 20 offers great hope for the future. But it also helps citizens of the kingdom to live contentedly, faithfully, and courageously under God's current, blessed reign.

---

26. Hendriksen, *Three Lectures*, 35.

CHAPTER 7

The Dead Will Rise

"Do you believe that after you die your physical body will be resurrected someday?" When asked that question a few years ago, only 36 percent of a large survey group answered "yes." By contrast 63 percent were "absolutely certain that Jesus died and physically rose from the dead." These statistics suggest that a strong majority of Americans believe that *Jesus* rose from the dead, but only a minority believe that *they* will experience a resurrection. More strikingly, less than 60 percent of evangelical Protestants who profess a "born again" faith have confidence in a personal resurrection. Albert Mohler, commenting on these numbers, says they are "…evidence of the doctrinal evasiveness of today's churches." He goes on to say that "the vast majority of Americans simply have no idea that the Bible clearly teaches a doctrine of personal resurrection and that the claim is central to the Gospel itself."[1]

The modern misunderstanding and underappreciation of the resurrection is a tragedy. If Christ is not raised, Christianity is empty because it cannot deliver the eternal, embodied lives that we desire (1 Cor. 15:14, 17). Those who adhere to the Christian

---

1. Al Mohler, "Do Christians Still Believe in the Resurrection of the Body?" *Albert Mohler* (blog), April 7, 2006, http://www.albertmohler.com/blog_read .php?id=600. Other polls show higher numbers of belief. "The Ipsos Reid survey (2006), commissioned by CanWest and Global News, found that a strong majority in both Canada (73%) and the United States (78%) indicated they believed Jesus Christ 'died on the cross and was resurrected to eternal life.'" http://www.lifesitenews.com/ldn/2006/apr/06041905.html.

religion without expecting a personal resurrection "are of all men the most pitiable" (v. 19).

Throughout Scripture, from Moses (Ex. 3:6; cf. Matt. 22:29–32), Job (Job 19:26), and David (2 Sam. 12:23) to Peter (1 Peter 1:3), Paul (Phil. 3:21), and Jesus (Luke 20:34–38), fellowship with God in resurrected bodies is the terminus of God's promise to be with His people. God's original approval of body-and-soul humans (Gen. 1:31) makes a strong point: full restoration from the fall has not happened until God's children enjoy intimate camaraderie with God and other humans *in the flesh*. The Bible's message of hope is grounded in the expectation of restored humanity, body and soul.

Will the Dead Rise?

The biblical doctrine of the resurrection has always been a cultural faux pas. The view of the ancient Greeks (Acts 17:32), the Sadducees contemporary with Jesus (Matt. 22:23; Acts 23:6–8), and modern materialists reflect the assumptions many people have about the life to come: either the spirit eternally outlives the body or both the spirit and body are destroyed at death. By contrast both the Old Testament (Isa. 26:19; Dan. 12:2–3) and especially the New Testament teach that at the return of Jesus, the bodies of all people will be re-created in order to stand before His seat of judgment.[2]

It is easy to understand why, when insisting on a doctrine that was unpopular (if not unheard of), misunderstood, counterintuitive, and foreign to experience, the biblical writers grounded the doctrine of the general resurrection in the resurrection of Jesus (see 1 Cor. 15:1–18). God has "begotten us again to a living hope through the resurrection of Jesus Christ from the dead"

---

2. While the Bible's emphasis is on the resurrection of the redeemed, it also insists that the unsaved too will stand before God in the flesh (Matt. 10:28; Mark 9:43–48; John 5:29).

(1 Peter 1:3). To Paul the resurrection of Christ was of first importance (1 Cor. 15:3).

In the classic text on the resurrection, 1 Corinthians 15, Paul both declares and defends the bodily resurrection of Jesus. His strongest proof is the testimony of still-living witnesses. The church at Corinth was quite removed from the events of Passion Week. Like subsequent Bible readers, many Corinthian Christians were Gentiles who had never been to Jerusalem and had never met Christ in the flesh. But Paul doesn't adjure them (or us) to believe that Christ had risen "because I told you so." For those interested in doing the research, hundreds of people could personally confirm that what Jesus announced beforehand had indeed come to pass: after dying, Christ arose (Matt. 20:19; cf. 27:63). These eyewitnesses saw Jesus of Nazareth— a man the Roman government confirmed to be dead (Mark 15:44–45)—walking, talking, eating, and teaching. Christ did not rise from the dead "in a corner" (Acts 26:23, 26)—in the shadows of obscurity—but on a political stage under Rome's watchful eye. Christ's death and resurrection were a "public spectacle" (Col. 2:15), an open-door triumph over the principalities and powers of darkness and death. To Paul, and many others of his day, denying the resurrection would have been as unseemly as denying the Holocaust, the stories of thousands of living witnesses notwithstanding.

Paul adds to the testimony of the eyewitnesses the changed lives of himself and the other apostles. Paul offers this puzzle over his changed behavior: how could a person who so vehemently "persecuted the church of God" now labor for Christ "more abundantly" than anyone else (1 Cor. 15:9–10)? The only solution is to grant that Jesus—whom Paul first believed to have died as an antichrist—appeared to him in the splendor of resurrection glory (Acts 26:12–18). The testimony of the other apostles was similar (cf. Luke 24:11 with Luke 24:36–42). Prior to the resurrection the disciples were fearful and reticent. After Jesus arose they

demonstrated unexpected boldness and faithfulness. Only the
resurrection can explain why Paul and the other disciples would
"stand in jeopardy every hour" (1 Cor. 15:30), dying daily (v. 31).

As further evidence Paul could have mentioned the various
resurrections in the Old Testament (1 Kings 17:21–22; 2 Kings
4:32–35; 13:21) and the New Testament (Matt. 27:50–53; Luke
8:49–56; John 11:38–44), the mystery of the empty tomb, the
otherwise inexplicable advance of the church, and the internal
testimony of the Holy Spirit.[3] Beyond reasonable doubt, "Christ
is risen from the dead and has become the firstfruits of those
who have fallen asleep" (1 Cor. 15:20).[4] As I write, in early spring
in the Midwest, most trees and shrubs have yet to bloom. But
some, like the forsythia, are a "first-fruit." Like Christ's resurrection, they pledge that a long, dark winter is almost over. A time
of new life is coming! This is the logic of Jesus's apostles. "If the
Spirit of Him who raised Jesus from the dead dwells in you, He
who raised Christ from the dead will also give life to your mortal
bodies through His Spirit who dwells in you" (Rom. 8:11). By
faith "we know that when He is revealed, we shall be like Him"
(1 John 3:2); He will "transform our lowly body that it may be
conformed to His glorious body" (Phil. 3:21).

How Will the Dead Rise?

The idea of a bodily resurrection seems a foreign concept. Calvin
admits, "There is nothing more at variance with human reason
than this article of faith."[5] And yet, says Paul, we see illustrations

---

3. See Calvin, *Institutes*, 1.7.4–5. For a brief elaboration on the biblical case for
the resurrection, see William Boekestein, "Defending the Resurrection," *Reformation 21* (blog), Alliance of Confessing Evangelicals, March 31, 2018, http://
www.reformation21.org/blog/2018/03/defending-the-resurrection.php.

4. For an excellent, brief defense of the resurrection see Timothy Keller, *The
Reason for God: Belief in an Age of Skepticism* (New York: Riverhead Books, 2008),
209–21.

5. John Calvin, *Commentary on the Epistles of Paul the Apostle to the Corinthians*
(Grand Rapids: Baker, 1989), 2:46.

of the resurrection all around us. A sort of resurrection happens every time a seed is planted. To those who make light of the resurrection on the ground that "resurrections don't happen," Paul is strong: "Foolish one, what you sow is not made alive unless it dies" (1 Cor. 15:36). For a seed to become a new plant it must not remain as a seed; it must decay and undergo a change in attributes. In the same way, for a human body to become something new it must not remain as it is. In the ordinary case, the body must die. It must be planted in the ground and decay. With this analogy Paul makes two main points.

Resurrection Bodies Will Be Similar to the Bodies of this Present Age

Paul writes, "To each seed its own body" (1 Cor. 15:38). The body, planted in the ground at death, is like a seed. The fully mature, flowering tree realized at the resurrection will be in every way superior to the seed, but it will be identifiably based on the template of the original body. A corn seed does not yield an oak tree. Christ's empty grave indicates the "substantial identity between His body that was buried and His resurrection body."[6]

To anticipate material from a later chapter, the continuity of resurrection bodies with our current "natural" bodies (v. 44) suggests also a great continuity in the age to come with the kinds of lives we live now. In the future age God's children will have eyes to take in the majesty of the new heavens and earth, ears to listen to the pleasant sounds of the restored creation, and hands and feet to cultivate the earth (see Gen. 2:5).

Resurrected Bodies Will Be Different from Bodies of This Present Age

The dead will be raised according to a change in attributes (1 Cor. 15:42–54). After Christ's resurrection His friends could still tell it was Him: "It is the Lord!" (John 21:7). But they could not doubt that He had changed. He now entered rooms through shut doors

---

6. Vos, *Redemptive History*, 320.

(John 20:26). Paul uses technical, often misunderstood language to describe this change. "The body is sown in corruption, it is raised in incorruption. It is sown in dishonor, it is raised in glory. It is sown in weakness, it is raised in power. It is sown a natural body, it is raised a spiritual body" (1 Cor. 15:42–44).

The contrast of which Paul speaks is precisely not between being physical and nonphysical. Paul's argument, in fact, is that in the age to come resurrected believers will be more truly physical than they are now, more well tuned to the multifaceted physicality of the world, like the body of the second Adam (v. 45). In this life, believers are governed by an ever-renewing spiritual life, but they do not have metamorphosed bodies to match. Presently believers live transformed spiritual lives in heavy, corrupted, dishonorable bodies. In the age to come believers' bodies, while physical, will be perfectly suited to their spiritual life in Christ. When Paul says that "flesh and blood cannot inherit the kingdom of God" (v. 50) he is not saying that believers will not have flesh and blood in the kingdom of the coming age. He's saying that our present bodies must "all be changed…corruptible must put on incorruption, and this mortal must put on immortality" (vv. 51, 53).

We need to be changed. We don't need to prove this. We get uncomfortable looking in a mirror; how could we look into the blazing majesty of God without first being changed? God's Old Testament demand of flawless sacrifices anticipated the spotless Lamb of God who would take away the sin of the world. But it also suggests the way in which God will transform—not only through sanctification, but much more through glorification—the bodies and souls of believers so that in the age to come they will have no "spot or wrinkle or any such…blemish" (Eph. 5:27). Jesus describes believers who have "attain[ed] that age, and the resurrection from the dead" as being "equal to the angels and are sons of God, being sons of the resurrection" (Luke 20:35–36). By this Jesus meant that resurrected bodies are not subject to decay nor are they able (for there is no need) to sexually reproduce.

Their very physical bodies will be perfectly suited to the blissful conditions of eternal shalom.

What Difference Does This Make?

The implications of the resurrection might seem obvious, but Paul ends his grand resurrection chapter with a few vital takeaways.

Believers Anticipate a Fully Embodied Eternity

Jesus's teaching on the resurrection "is shaped by one great principle, that the kingdom of God and the salvation it brings cannot stop short of the complete reclaiming of men, *body as well as soul*, from death, nor of their complete equipment for the consummate fellowship with God in heaven."[7] God's promise of eternal fellowship is made to humans, not merely to souls. The deep desire of humanity—and the culmination of God's promise—is to commune with God to the fullest capacity of our humanity. The fulfillment of this promise requires resurrected bodies. Vos writes, "The raising of the body marks, as it were, the final admission of the completely restored man into the enjoyment of the fatherly love of God."[8]

The Resurrection Removes Death's Sting and Cancels the Grave's Victory

Death leaves a permanent sting when it strikes a person who seemed to have no interest in Christ and no known aspirations for eternal fellowship with God. Hollow indeed is the sound of earth striking the vault containing the remains of a person who left this life negligent of God's will for happily entering the life to come. Hades seems victorious.

But when Paul writes about God's promise to resurrect the bodies of believers he describes it as a victory over death (1 Cor. 15:54), an annulling of death's victory (v. 55). Christ came to earth

---

7. Vos, *Redemptive History*, 320.
8. Vos, *Redemptive History*, 320.

to subdue enemies and make right those things which are out of order in God's world, the last of which is death (1 Cor. 15:26). In some ways Christ has already put death under His feet. He has conquered it in His own resurrection. He has turned death into the servant of believers; death for believers is a sort of resurrection, an "entering into eternal life."[9] When Christ returns, death itself will be no more.

The Resurrection Steels Believers to Persevere in Meaningful Labor

Because of the resurrection life that Christ brings, all of our actions have implications that outlast this life. The resurrection rescues believers from the fear that our very mundane tasks are nothing but vanity (1 Cor. 15:58). In the age to come, saints will rest "from their labors" but "their works follow them" (Rev. 14:13). The resurrection urges us to pursue the myriad activities we can do "in the Lord" while avoiding works that are truly vain.

The Resurrection Teaches Believers to Practice the Art of Celebration

Solomon's tentative conclusion that "nothing is better for a man than that he should eat and drink, and that his soul should enjoy good in his labor" (Eccl. 2:24) might sound faulty to us. After all, we've read Paul's reflection on Solomon. "If the dead do not rise, 'Let us eat and drink, for tomorrow we die'" (1 Cor. 15:32). But Paul isn't contradicting Solomon. He's simply saying that celebration would be the *only* thing to do if there were no resurrection. The unbeliever's grossly incomparable alternative to a good resurrection is earthly feasting. For the believer a proper celebration of God's good gifts is a prelude to the resurrection which Scripture routinely describes as a party (or, if you prefer, a banquet). Jesus previews the Lamb's marriage supper (Rev. 19:9) by creating superlative wine at an earthly wedding party (John 2:1–12).

---

9. HC 42; cf. John 5:24; Rom. 7:24–25; Phil. 1:23.

Those who believe in the resurrection should be pacesetters in God-honoring celebration.

> Modern man…always keeps on believing that the real thing is going to happen tomorrow. In this kind of life the past has degenerated into a series of used or misused opportunities, the present into a constant concern about accomplishments, and the future into a make-believe paradise where man hopes to finally receive what he always wanted but the existence of which he basically doubts. A life like this cannot be celebrated because we're constantly concerned with changing it into something else, always trying to do something to it, get something out of it, and make it fit our many plans and projects.[10]

The promise of the resurrection frees us from the impossible pressure of creating a utopia now and frees us to practice biblically moderated celebration, not as self-worship but as a beautiful human expression of glorifying the God of resurrection (1 Cor. 10:31).

One day our flesh and blood will be reunited to the earth; we all will either gradually wear out or die suddenly and unexpectedly. The only suitable salvation from that state is the very redemption promised in Scripture: the resurrection of the body.

---

10. Henri J. Nouwen, *Creative Ministry: Beyond Professionalism in Teaching, Preaching, Counseling, Organizing and Celebrating* (New York: Doubleday, 1971), 99.

CHAPTER 8

The Final Judgment

There are few less popular emphases in Christianity today than that of judgment. The church, the Bible, and even God Himself seem given to a policy of discrimination against those who might not even share a common standard of conduct. Nowhere is Christianity's "judgmentalism" seen more sharply than in the doctrine of final judgment. To many, the conclusion of one of Jesus's final parables is perniciously obnoxious: the wicked "will go away into everlasting punishment, but the righteous into eternal life" (Matt. 25:46).

At first glance any notion of judgment seems very unwelcome; we want to believe and behave without censure or consequence. Judgment is unwelcome *until* we need our day in court. When a district attorney pledges to bring a serial rapist to justice, nobody says, "Don't judge." The quest of all people to be vindicated—our desire for vengeance when we've been wronged and our pleas for leniency when we've been wrong—testifies to a grander scheme of morality. Our inner delight in justice—though often fueled by selfishness and betraying gross inconsistency—is irrepressible.

Christians naturally accept Christ's prerogative to judge the world. For two millennia believers have expressed this biblical truth: Christ is coming again to judge the living and the dead. But non-Christians too can easily reason that *if there is a God* "who made the world and everything in it," including "every nation of men," and if He has determined that "they should seek the Lord…and find Him," then He has every right to appoint a day on which to "judge the world in righteousness by the Man whom He has ordained" (Acts 17:24–31). This is exactly Paul's message to a non-Christian audience in Athens. Paul could have added that if this God wanted to assure His creatures that He was fully capable of judging the human condition, it would make sense for Him to walk this earth in human flesh, experiencing unkindness, oppression, and injustice firsthand. To fully appreciate inequity it would be good for Him to be arraigned by jealous prosecutors using fallacious evidence, condemned by a dishonest judge, and publicly executed for crimes He didn't commit. Such was the experience of Jesus. Paul does say this: God "has given assurance of this [day of judgment] to all by raising Him from the dead" (v. 31).[1]

The Bible's Program for Final Judgment

Scripture communicates a very simple program for the conquest of justice.

Under God's superintendence a "shadow" of justice operates now. God often uses human instruments "to execute wrath on him who practices evil" (Rom. 13:4). At the end of this present age, justice will "run down like water, and righteousness like a mighty stream" (Amos 5:24). On that day not everyone shall enter the kingdom of heaven. The Father has given authority to the Son to "execute judgment…for the hour is coming in which all who are in the graves will hear His voice and come forth" (John 5:27–29). Those who acted justly, loved mercy, and walked humbly with their God (Mic. 6:8) will be raised to life and hear Jesus say, "Come, you blessed of My Father, inherit the kingdom prepared for you from the foundation of the world" (Matt. 25:34). On the

---

1. Interestingly, the judgment part of Paul's speech seemed to resonate with the law-conscious Romans. It was the resurrection for which they had no category (see v. 32).

same day, those who have done evil, "ungodly men" will taste the "resurrection of condemnation" and enter into "perdition" (John 5:27–29; 2 Peter 3:7). Those who had practiced lawlessness will be sent away from God's good presence (Matt. 7:21–23).

On that day even the heavens and earth will be judged and given over to purifying fire (2 Peter 3:7). The heavens and earth will be remade into a dwelling place for God's redeemed people while the rest remain outside the city gates (Rev. 22:15).[2]

The Reason for Final Judgment

The Day of Judgment Glorifies Christ

The day of judgment is rightly called the day of the Lord (Acts 2:20) because on that day, as never before, God will be all in all (1 Cor. 15:28). The judgment is committed to Christ "as one of the crowning honors of his kingship."[3] He will judge—finally and fully—every power that has challenged His majesty, including fallen angels, the devil, and his demons. The final judgment is a vindication of God which will display before "all rational creatures the declarative glory of God in a formal, forensic act, which magnifies on the one hand His holiness and righteousness, and on the other hand His grace and mercy."[4] On that day "every knee should bow…and…every tongue…confess that Jesus Christ is Lord, to the glory of God the Father" (Phil. 2:10–11). Thomas Watson wrote that at the final judgment, "sinners will be so clearly convicted that they shall hold up their hand at the bar

---

2. On the "outside-ness" of hell, C. S. Lewis observes, "We know much more about heaven than hell, for heaven is the home of humanity and therefore contains all that is implied in a glorified human life: but hell was not made for men. It is in no sense *parallel* to heaven: it is 'the darkness outside,' the outer rim where being fades away into nonentity." C. S. Lewis, *The Problem of Pain*, in *The C. S. Lewis Signature Classics* (New York: HarperCollins, 2017), 626.

3. Berkhof, *Systematic Theology*, 732.

4. Berkhof, *Systematic Theology*, 731. Cf. the Westminster Confession of Faith (henceforth WCF) 33.2.

and cry 'guilty'…the sinner himself shall clear God of injustice."[5] Every sin of believers will be publicly pardoned for Jesus's sake. Christ's reward to believers (Matt. 25:34; 2 John 1:8) will unquestionably testify of God's amazing, unmerited favor. As Matthew Henry wrote, the reward for the works of believers "will be far above the merit of all their services and sufferings."[6]

The Day of Judgment Warns Unbelievers

Pending judgment is a threat to the guilty. Jesus often described the day of judgment as a warning against religious people who reject His invitation to enter His kingdom (Matt. 10:5–15), ignore His mighty works (Matt. 11:20–24), and fail to bear good fruit (Matt. 12:33–37). The day of judgment is especially for the "unjust…who walk according to the flesh in the lust of uncleanness and despise authority. They are presumptuous, self-willed" (2 Peter 2:9–10). Paul warns those who have hard and impenitent hearts: "You are treasuring up for yourself wrath in the day of wrath and revelation of the righteous judgment of God, who 'will render to each one according to his deeds'…to those who are self-seeking and do not obey the truth, but obey unrighteousness—indignation and wrath, tribulation and anguish, on every soul of man who does evil" (Rom. 2:5–9). Jesus commanded the apostles "to preach to the people, and to testify that it is He who was ordained by God to be Judge of the living and the dead" (Acts 10:34–43). Those who "destroy the earth" shall be destroyed by God's anger in the judgment (Rev. 11:18).

Coupled with this warning is an invitation: "Cast away from you all the transgressions which you have committed, and get yourselves a new heart and a new spirit. For why should you

---

5. Thomas Watson, *The Duty of Self-Denial: And Ten Other Sermons* (Grand Rapids: Reformation Heritage Books, 1997), 173. See also Jude 14–15: "Behold, the Lord comes…to execute judgment on all, to convict all who are ungodly among them of all their ungodly deeds."

6. Henry, *Commentary on the Whole Bible*, 1:1166.

die?" (Ezek. 18:31). The age leading up to the final judgment is a time of grace in which God refrains from judgment, showcasing His "goodness, forbearance, and longsuffering" so that people would repent and be saved from the coming wrath (Rom. 2:4).

Pending Judgment Comforts the Pardoned

Even an innocent person might feel anxious about going to court and standing before a judge. So too, Christians might fear to stand before God's "great white throne" and Him who sits on it, "from whose face the earth and the heaven" fly away (Rev. 20:11). To assuage our fears John Calvin asks the following pastoral questions: "How could a most merciful prince destroy his own people? How could the head disperse its own members? How could the advocate condemn his clients?"[7] The judge of believers is the "very One who has already stood trial in [their] place before God and so has removed the whole curse from [them]."[8] Because there is "no condemnation to those who are in Christ Jesus" (Rom. 8:1), to those among whom "love has been perfected," believers "may have boldness in the day of judgment; because as He is, so are we in this world" (1 John 4:17). By faith in the Son of God, believers have "already, under the soteriological regime of grace, received absolute, eternal acquittal in justification."[9] To "those who have loved His appearing," Christ, the righteous Judge, will certainly give a "crown of righteousness" (2 Tim. 4:8). God can disapprove of some of the works of His children (1 Cor. 3:15) and still judge them kindly on the basis of the merits of Jesus's faithfulness.

The Westminster Confession of Faith ends on this urgent note: "As Christ would have us to be certainly persuaded that there shall be a day of judgment, both to deter all men from sin; and for the greater consolation of the godly in their adversity (2 Peter 3:11, 14; 2 Cor. 5:10–11; 2 Thess. 1:5–7; Luke 21:7, 28;

---

7. Calvin, *Institutes*, 2.16.18.
8. HC 52.
9. Vos, *Redemptive History*, 52.

Rom. 8:23–25): so will He have that day unknown to men, that they may shake off all carnal security, and be always watchful, because they know not at what hour the Lord will come; and may be ever prepared to say, Come Lord Jesus, come quickly. Amen (Matt. 24:36, 42–44; Mark 13:35–37; Luke 12:35–36; Rev. 22:20)."[10]

The Cosmic Implications of Final Judgment

The earth was cursed because of the sin of man (Gen. 3:17–19). In the same way, the earth's hope for renewal is tied to the renewal of her keepers, God's people. Like men, "heaven and earth will pass away" (Luke 21:33). But, as with God's judgment against people, the judgment against the world is not an annihilation of the world.[11] Peter, writing to correct those who scoff that "all things continue as they were from the beginning of creation," compares the deluge of the ancient world (Genesis 7) with the burning of the present world at the last day (2 Peter 3:6–13). According to Peter "the world that then existed perished, being flooded with water" (v. 6), that is, "the continuity of nature, was broken up by the flood."[12] As the Belgic Confession explains, "the world that perished is said to be a different world from that which rose out of the flood, not by a reduction to nothing, but by a [purging]."[13]

---

10. WCF 33.3.

11. "We maintain that there will be a change of the world and a change by which the creature will be delivered from the bondage of corruption and which assuredly will not be an annihilation, but rather a restoration…and renewal." Francis Turretin, *Institutes of Elenctic Theology* (Phillipsburg, N.J.: P&R, 1997), 596. Turretin admits, however, that "this question is problematical and of the number of those in which it is lawful to hold ourselves back…and to differ (truth and charity being preserved)," 590.

12. Michael Green, *The Second Epistle General of Peter and the General Epistle of Jude: An Introductory Commentary*, Tyndale New Testament Commentaries (Grand Rapids: Eerdmans, 1999), 142.

13. Turretin, *Institutes*, 591.

The fires of the last judgment "cleanse" this "old world."[14] So it will be at the last day.

We often impulsively imagine that fire is only destructive, especially when the Bible uses it to describe a judgment. But fire is also a means of renewal; one of the best ways to rid a property of unusable bramble and to prepare the earth for new growth is a controlled burn. Scripture elsewhere describes the destruction of this earth as "regeneration" (Matt. 19:28) and a "restoration" (Acts 3:21). The "whole creation groans and labors," says Paul, not to be annihilated but to give birth to something new. So creation will be "delivered from the bondage of corruption into…glorious liberty" (Rom. 8:22, 21). The psalmist wrote that God will change the heavens and earth like a garment that has grown old; they will not be destroyed but "they will be changed" (Ps. 102:25–26). Luther put it this way, today "the heavens have their work-day clothes on; hereafter they will have on their Sunday garments."[15] When God re-forms[16] the new heavens and a new earth, they will be so superior to the old that "the former shall not be remembered or come to mind" (Isa. 65:17).

To illustrate this thorough transformation, Scripture uses the eschatological category of "new heavens" and "new earth" (2 Peter 3:13) as if it were a single new creation, mirroring the God-indwelt world of Genesis 1. The phrase portrays the coming together of the special sphere of men and the special sphere of God in answer to the words Jesus taught His people to pray: "Your kingdom come. Your will be done on earth as it is in heaven" (Matt. 6:10). That these two spheres should become one, though still called by two names, is perfectly consistent with the

---

14. BC 37.

15. Quoted in Charles Hodge, *Systematic Theology* (Grand Rapids: Eerdmans, 1975), 3:853.

16. Isaiah's verb *bara* can mean "to create out of nothing" or "to fashion from existing materials," as was the case when God created Adam from the dust of the earth (Gen. 1:27, cf. Gen. 2:7).

fact that the restored dwelling place of God has many names: the New Jerusalem (Rev. 21:2), Mount Zion (Rev. 14:1), the heavenly Jerusalem (Heb. 12:22), the city of God (Ps. 46:4; 87:3). When God makes all things new (Rev. 21:5), the New Jerusalem will come "down out of heaven from God, prepared as a bride adorned for her husband." John heard a voice speaking about that day: "'Behold the tabernacle of God is with men, and He will dwell with them, and they shall be His people. God Himself will be with them and be their God'" (Rev. 21:2–3).

Appropriate Reactions to Final Judgment

Trust God to Do What Is Right

The great existential problem many people face in reflecting on the final judgment is that it necessarily leaves some people out. Berkhof writes, "For all those who appear in judgment entrance into, or exclusion from, heaven, will depend on the question, whether they are clothed with the righteousness of Jesus Christ."[17] And Paul bluntly observes, "Not all have faith" (2 Thess. 3:2). But the Bible does not insist that explicit, self-conscious faith in Christ is necessary to endure the judgment.[18] Precisely how God will judge those who did not live long enough to believe, who lacked the capacity for conscious faith, or who lacked any access to the gospel is not told us. "Whatever God *might choose to do* in any given case, he has promised to save all of those—and only those—who call on the name of his Son." Still, "it is precisely because God is sovereign and free in his grace that he can have mercy on whomever he chooses."[19] He who knows the bitterness of false judgment can be trusted to judge fairly. Indeed, the Judge of all the earth shall do right (Gen. 18:25). The avenger of the

---

17. Berkhof, *Systematic Theology*, 733.
18. Horton, *Christian Faith*, 983.
19. Horton, *Christian Faith*, 983.

poor and the persecuted (Ps. 109:31, cf. Deut. 15:11) will not err on the great day.

Exercise Modesty in Judging Others

God's abeyance of the judgment until the last day (Matt. 13:37–43) should caution believers about judging others hastily (1 Cor. 4:5). Paul says that believers will judge the world (1 Cor. 6:2; Ps. 49:14), but only after the dimness is removed from our eyes and we will know with a perception now unfathomed (1 Cor. 13:12). In the meantime, in light of the fact that "we shall all stand before the judgment seat of Christ…let us not judge one another anymore, but rather resolve this, not to put a stumbling block or a cause to fall in our brother's way" (Rom. 14:10–13).[20] The final judgment helps us especially resist the judgment of vengeance. Keller writes, "If we have known real evil, we will want a divine judge who will take up the sword, so that we can refrain from doing so."[21] If we truly understand the dreadfulness of falling into the hands of the living God (Heb. 10:31) we will not avenge ourselves but rather give place to the wrath of God (Rom. 12:17–19). Today is the day not for praying spiteful curses against those who curse us but "the time of prayer for our enemies and bringing the good news to the ends of the earth" (Matt. 5:43–44).[22]

---

20. These cautions do not contradict Scripture's command that believers judge "with righteous judgment," or that church leaders exercise careful judgment in matters of church discipline (Matt. 16:19; 18:17–18) and in lieu of civil litigation between brothers (1 Cor. 6:1–6). They do, however, urge us to follow Jesus's example in committing ourselves to Him who judges righteously (1 Peter 2:21–23).

21. Timothy Keller, *The Songs of Jesus: A Year of Daily Devotionals in the Psalms* (New York: Viking, 2015), 124. Cf. Timothy Keller, *The Reason for God: Belief in an Age of Skepticism* (New York: Riverhead Books, 2008), 76–78.

22. Michael Horton, "Should Christians Pray for God to Judge Their Enemies?," Core Christianity, Nov. 17, 2017, https://corechristianity.com/resource-library/articles/should-christians-pray-for-god-to-judge-their-enemies.

Live Circumspectly

Believers are forever free from the condemnation of God (John 3:18). This profound reality promotes a careful piety, a commitment to walk in the light that our "deeds may be clearly seen, that they have been done in God" (John 3:21). To the redeemed believer every deed matters, even our pre-deeds; God discerns even the secret "thoughts and intents of the heart" (Heb. 4:12). Believers recognize that they will stand in the judgment individually, not based on family connections or the orthodoxy of the church they had attended. "Each of us shall give account of himself to God" (Rom. 14:12). The careful piety of the final-judgment-conscious believer does not, however, degrade his concept of God's love. In fact, it is the very opposite! It was expressly during the Reformation, under the ministry of the gospel, that Christian people were delivered from a pervasive, even oppressive, sense that God is *only* a judge, or a judge without feeling, without love. Because God loves His children with a never-ending, sacrificial affection, the final judgment can deepen our trust in Him, helping the believer to say, "In all my sorrows and persecutions, I, with uplifted head look for the very One, who offered Himself for me to the judgment of God, and removed all curse from me, to come as Judge from heaven (Luke 21:28; Rom. 8:23–24; Phil. 3:20–21; Titus 2:13), who shall cast all His and my enemies into everlasting condemnation (2 Thess. 1:6–10; Matt. 25:41), but shall take me with all His chosen ones to Himself into heavenly joy and glory."[23]

---

23. HC 52.

CHAPTER 9

Hell

One recent book on hell begins with this line: "If you are excited to read this book, you have issues." The authors later add, "Hell should not be studied without tearful prayer."[1] Paul Helm writes similarly, "Hell is a dreadful topic, which anyone with any sensitivity naturally shrinks from thinking about." It is appropriate to not like hell. In fact, we can be stronger: it is *not right* to savor thoughts of eternal punishment.

"And yet," adds Helm, "a certain type of religious personality has loved to dwell on the subject, to embellish it in lurid detail, to linger on the pains, and the hopelessness, in a way that tells us more about such a person's own psychological and spiritual state than about the sober and restrained witness of Scripture."[2]

Those who delight in the topic of hell or who love to emphasize hell beyond biblical warrant betray hearts that poorly reflect the attitude of God on the topic. At the tomb of Lazarus, Jesus wept (John 11:17–37). Of course—He loved His dead friend. But He also wept over the hardness of heart of the unbelievers at that funeral. Jesus cried because He knew that for some in that crowd,

---

1. Francis Chan and Preston Sprinkle, *Erasing Hell: What God Said about Eternity, and the Things We've Made Up* (Colorado Springs: David C. Cook, 2011), 11, 17.

2. Paul Helm, *The Last Things: Death, Judgment, Heaven, Hell* (Edinburgh: Banner of Truth, 1989), 108. Herman Bavinck, along with a host of other thoughtful theologians, agreed: "It must be noted that this doctrine…is often depicted in too much realistic detail in the church and in theology." *Last Things*, 148.

He would not be the resurrection and the life. As He looked toward the gaping mouth of the cave of Lazarus's tomb, perhaps Christ thought of that "bottomless pit" out of which smoke, as of a great furnace, always arises (Rev. 9:2) into which all rebellious creatures will one day be cast. Later Jesus wailed over Jerusalem, over the scores of hard-hearted people who rejected His offer of refuge (Luke 13:34). God does not love hell; He does not delight in the destruction of the wicked (Ezek. 18:23).

Besides being symptomatic of a shrunken heart, imaginative, lurid, and eager descriptions of hell can needlessly hinder others from embracing the Bible and its Author. C. S. Lewis was bluntly honest about hell: "There is no doctrine which I would more willingly remove from Christianity than this, if it lay in my power." But Lewis was well aware that his disdain of hell could not change reality. The doctrine of hell, he acknowledged, "has the full support of Scripture and, specially, of our Lord's own words; it has always been held by Christendom; and it has the support of reason."[3] With only few, radical exceptions throughout history, the church has understood the Bible to teach the reality of a place called hell.

The Testimony of Scripture

Studying what the Bible says about hell can try one's faith.[4] What we do with the subject "is a litmus test of our readiness to follow the way set out in the Scriptures, even when the way proves difficult."[5]

---

3. C.S. Lewis, *The Problem of Pain,* in *The C.S. Lewis Signature Classics* (New York: HarperCollins, 2017), 620–21.

4. J. I. Packer's 1990 "Leon Morris Essay" addresses his concern that "the divinely executed retributive process that operates in the world to come is becoming more and more a problem area for belief." "The Problem of Eternal Punishment," *Crux* 26, no. 3 (Sept. 1990): 18–25.

5. Venema, *Christ and the Future,* 202.

At the same time, we must resist the temptation to hyper-literalize the Bible's descriptions of hell, as if orthodoxy demanded a commitment to the most ghastly interpretation of the verses in question. Louis Berkhof is helpful at this point: "It is undoubtedly true…that a great deal of the language concerning heaven and hell must be understood figuratively."[6] Accepting a nonliteral understanding of hell's images is not a soft-peddling of Scripture. Charles Hodge explains, "These descriptions of the judgment are designed to teach us moral truths, and not the physical phenomena" by which God's judgment will be accomplished. The temperature of hell and its precise location "are questions about which we need give ourselves no concern."[7] Modern Reformed theologians agree. Venema writes, "Biblical imagery conveys something of the reality of hell, but ought not be taken literally. We should think soberly and carefully about the reality to which this imagery points us: the reality of being banished from the blessed presence of God, being under the felt impression of his everlasting displeasure, and being subjected to the perpetual frustration and fury of sinful, but futile, rebellion against his will."[8] It is, in fact, "impossible to determine precisely what will constitute the eternal punishment of the wicked, and it behooves us to speak very cautiously on the subject."[9]

Sincere readers recognize that hell, despite its offensiveness, is not a fringe topic of Scripture. Rather, it is at the center of the warnings of Jesus and the apostles; it functions the same in the Old Testament as in the New. The message of Scripture about hell can be simply summarized in a brief sentence: hell is a place of unending negative judgment against the unsaved, commencing after Christ's return.

---

6. Berkhof, *Systematic Theology*, 736.
7. Charles Hodge, *Systematic Theology* (Grand Rapids: Eerdmans, 1975), 3:849.
8. Venema, *Christ and the Future*, 202–3. Cf. Horton, *Christian Faith*, 976.
9. Berhkof, *Systematic Theology*, 736.

Hell Is a Place

As critics of a literal hell suggest, there is surely a sense in which "hell is now." Bavinck writes, "Aside from Scripture there is no stronger proof for the existence of hell than the existence of this world…from whose misery the features of the [biblical] picture of hell are derived."[10] But while consistently and candidly acknowledging the hellish conditions which sin creates in this present age, the Bible is clear: hell, as a dwelling place for unsaved humans and fallen angels, is primarily *coming*. People can enter, or more forcibly, be cast into hell (Matt. 5:29–30, 18:8–9; Luke 12:5). Hell is described as a place with boundaries that cannot be crossed (Luke 16:26). Those who affirm the reality of heaven should, with trembling honesty, do the same for hell.[11]

Hell Is a Place of Negative Judgment

Hell is a place of gloomy darkness (2 Peter 2:4 ESV) in which one's soul and body experience a sort of death (Matt. 10:28). It is a place of punishment, destruction, and privation.[12] Hell is, in fact, synonymous with destruction (Prov. 15:11). It is contrasted with the place of life (Prov. 15:24). God's presence in hell is as the eternal Judge, devoid of any blessed manifestations of His love, mercy, and grace (Ps. 139:8).[13]

Hell Is a Place of Unending Negative Judgment

By appealing either to Scripture or to a certain sense of God's character—or as a way of avoiding the crushing weight of the

---

10. Bavinck, *Last Things*, 152.

11. Rob Bell, for example, inconsistently affirms that heaven is a real "place, space, and dimension" but claims that hell is "a big, wide, terrible evil that comes from the secrets hidden deep within our hearts all the way to the massive, society-wide collapse and chaos that comes when we fail to live in God's world God's way." *Love Wins: A Book about Heaven, Hell, and the Fate of Every Person Who Ever Lived* (New York: HarperCollins, 2011), 42, 93.

12. Lewis, *Problem of Pain*, 624.

13. See Michael Horton, "Hell Is Not Separation from God," *Core Christianity*, Dec. 28, 2017, https://corechristianity.com/resource-library/articles/hell-is-not-separation-from-god.

alternative—some Christians have suggested that hell is merely a symbol for the total annihilation of unbelievers occurring at or after the final judgment. In its various forms annihilationism, or conditional immortality, teaches that there is no hell in which the damned experience eternal conscious punishment.[14] Against this view, Scripture uses the same word (OT: *olam*; NT: *aionios*) to describe the eternal punishment of the wicked and the eternal life of the righteous (Dan. 12:2; Matt. 25:46). Four times in a brief speech Jesus repeats this grim reality: hell's fires shall never be quenched (Mark 9:43–48). As Charles Hodge says, God "has never, either in his word or in his works, revealed his purpose to destroy anything He has once created."[15] God's prophets, and none more so than Jesus, warn against hell because hell is a place of never-ending loss, not merely a state of nonbeing.

Hell Is a Place of Unending Judgment against the Unsaved

Hell is a place for those from all nations who refused to submit to the Lord in this life, but instead worshiped the devil and his demons (Rev. 14:8–10). The doom of some ungodly men "who long ago were marked out for this condemnation" is certain (Jude 4).

At the same time, says Bavinck, "In light of Scripture, both with regard to the salvation of pagans and that of children who die in infancy, we cannot get beyond abstaining from a firm judgment, in either a positive or a negative sense."[16] Other Reformed theologians have been even more optimistic: on the basis of God's electing grace, "we have reason to believe...that the number of the finally lost in comparison with the whole number of

---

14. Conditional immortality is the belief that "man was created mortal, and that immortality is a gift which God confers as a reward upon the righteous, although some have held that man was created immortal but that the wicked are, by a positive act of God, deprived of that gift." Loraine Boettner, *Immortality* (Philadelphia: Presbyterian and Reformed, 1956), 117.

15. Hodge, *Systematic Theology*, 3:852.

16. Bavinck, *Last Things*, 165.

the saved will be very inconsiderable. Our blessed Lord, when surrounded by the innumerable company of the redeemed, will be hailed as the…Savior of Men, as the Lamb that bore the sins of the world."[17] "In the lack of people is the downfall of a prince" (Prov. 14:28). Will God have such a problem? Will He not be honored by a multitude?

The Bible is clear: there is a hell and it is a place to be avoided, literally, at all costs (Matt. 16:26). Still, what Charles Hodge says of the final judgment is sound advice for all contemplation of the future. The diverse and often unexpected ways God has fulfilled past promises "should render us modest in our interpretation of those predictions which remain to be accomplished; satisfied that what we know not now we shall know hereafter."[18] Notably, the Reformers, their confessions, and those who follow in their footsteps, offer few details about the judgment or the particulars of hell. They summarize the consistent but often nonspecific data of Scripture but go no further.

---

17. Hodge, *Systematic Theology*, 3:879–80. B. B. Warfield also affirms that "the number of the saved shall in the end be not small but large, and not merely absolutely but comparatively large; …to speak plainly, it shall embrace the immensely greater part of the human race." "Are They Few that Be Saved?" in *Biblical and Theological Studies*, ed. Samuel G. Craig (Philadelphia: Presbyterian and Reformed, 1968), 349. In this essay Warfield argues that the texts (e.g., Matt. 7:13–14) frequently adduced to sustain the argument that the total number elected are few, in fact merely reflect the situation of pervasive unbelief current in Jesus's day. Most pointedly, they urge the hearers not to prognosticate about the proportion of the elect but that "salvation is difficult and that it is our duty to address ourselves to obtaining it with diligence and earnest effort." He adds, "We can never learn" from these texts "how many are saved" (338). On a related text, Matthew 22:14, Calvin recognizes that while the apparent ratio of saved to unsaved persons varies throughout the ages, Jesus's words, "For many are called, but few are chosen" ought not prompt us to "enter…into the question about the eternal election of God." *Commentary on a Harmony of the Evangelists, Matthew, Mark, and Luke* (Grand Rapids: Baker, 1989), 2:175.

18. Hodge, *Systematic Theology*, 3:850–51.

The Justice of Hell

We struggle to see how hell can be an expression of God's justice, in part "because we have preconceptions, anticipations of what hell must be like, drawn from fiction or from our own imagination. But the Bible—Christ Himself—offers a particular warning about entertaining such preconceptions, as if it were obvious now who will be in hell and who not! (Mark 10:31).... Scripture goes as far as to say that the Day of Judgment will bring surprises" (Luke 13:23–30).[19] Hell is not a "torture chamber, nor an Inquisition," for everyone who believes differently than us, "but a place of justice" under the watchful care of a perfectly just God.[20]

God's judgment of hell is just, as J. I. Packer notes, for two reasons. First, "what people receive is not only what they deserve but what they have in effect already chosen—namely to be without God and therefore without any of the good that he gives; second, the fact that the sentence is proportioned to the knowledge of God's word, work, and will that was actually disregarded" (cf. Luke 12:42–48; Rom. 1:18–20, 32; 2:4, 12–15).[21]

Hell Is a Chosen Destiny

Paul says of those who actively "suppress the truth in unrighteousness" that "God also gave them up to uncleanness, in the lusts of their hearts...who exchanged the truth of God for the lie.... For this reason God gave them up" (Rom. 1:18, 24–26). J. I. Packer, in critiquing the annihilationist position, says, "There is no reason to think that the resurrection of the lost for judgment will change their character, and every reason therefore to suppose that their rebellion and impenitence will continue as long as they themselves do, making continued banishment from

---

19. Helm, *Last Things*, 112.

20. Helm, *Last Things*, 110.

21. J. I. Packer, "Evangelical Annihilationism in Review," *Reformation & Revival*, 6, no. 2 (Spring 1997): 42.

God's fellowship fully appropriate."[22] C. S. Lewis also interacts with this notion. "I willingly believe that the damned are, in one sense, successful rebels to the end; that the doors of hell are locked on the *inside*.... They enjoy forever the horrible freedom that they have demanded, and are therefore self-enslaved: just as the blessed, forever submitting to obedience, become through all eternity more and more free."[23]

A Proportionate Destiny

Several Scripture passages counter the notion that everyone in hell will face identical eternities. Rather, "there will be different degrees, both of the bliss of heaven and of the punishment of hell," such that hell will be more tolerable for some than for others (Matt. 10:15; Luke 10:14; 12:47–48; John 9:39–41; Rom. 2:12–16; James 4:17).[24] Bavinck writes, "The penalty of damnation (*poena damni*) is the same, but the penalty of sensation (*poena sensus*) differs."[25] The Bible gives us no grounds to imagine a respectable nonbeliever suffering an identical fate with the most evil dictator. As Helm says, "If...none suffer there except those who deserve to suffer, and none suffer more, nor less, than they deserve, then hell is not evil."[26]

A Dehumanizing Destiny

Charles Hodge points out that "as long as rational creatures are sinful, they must be degraded and miserable."[27] He suggests that sin, and therefore, especially never-ending sinning, reduces the quality of humanity and the image of God in man. We cannot even say with certainty that the damned will "possess the qualities

---

22. Packer, "Evangelical Annihilationism," 46.
23. Lewis, *Problem of Pain*, 626.
24. Berkhof, *Systematic Theology*, 733. See also P. Y. DeJong, *The Church's Witness to the World* (Pella, Iowa: Pella Publishing, 1962), 2:429.
25. Bavinck, *Last Things*, 154.
26. Helm, *Last Things*, 114.
27. Hodge, *Systematic Theology*, 3:879.

of the glorified body like the elect."[28] C. S. Lewis suggests that "to enter heaven is to become more human than you ever succeeded in being on earth; to enter hell, is to be banished from humanity. What is cast (or casts itself) into hell is not a man: it is 'remains.'"[29] The Scripture says this of idolaters: "They followed vanity and became vain" (2 Kings 17:15 NASB). B. B. Warfield describes a view of eternal punishment in which those who enter hell are transformed by the degrading character of sin and the absence of God's common grace "into a condition below the possibility of any moral action or moral concern…like persons in life whose personality is entirely overwhelmed by the base sense of what we call physical fear."[30] William Hendriksen says that the lost "sink *away* endlessly *from* the presence of God and of the lamb" into what J. I. Packer calls "introversion to the point of idiocy."[31]

The Bible's "Use" of Hell

Without question, the Bible writers talk about hell not for the purpose of sadistic speculation nor to frighten those who have accepted Jesus's invitation to find rest in Him (Matt. 11:28–30). While hell is entirely negative, the doctrine is meant to be used positively.

Hell Urges Us to Fight against Sin

Sin always brings misery. When nurtured and cultivated sin grows into a sort of hell, life with all the best parts sucked out. For this

---

28. The Hungarian Confessio Catholica, 2:625.

29. Lewis, *Problem of Pain*, 625. The arguments against an "equal ultimacy" between divine election and reprobation are helpful in dismissing a view that hell is a perfect negative of heaven. See Fred H. Klooster, *Calvin's Doctrine of Predestination*, Calvin Theological Seminary Monograph Series: III (Grand Rapids: Calvin Theological Seminary, 1961), 47–54.

30. Samuel Macauley Jackson, ed., *The New Schaff-Herzog Encyclopedia of Religious Knowledge* (New York: Funk and Wagnalls, 1908), s.v. "Annihilationism," by B. B. Warfield.

31. William Hendriksen, *The Bible on the Life Hereafter* (Grand Rapids: Baker, 1959), 201. Packer, "The Problem of Eternal Punishment," 25.

reason, hell is even—*especially*—a warning to religious people who know better about sin and judgment. Jesus was intentionally provocative on this point: very religious people can go to hell (Matt. 7:21–23; 23:15). Fighting against sin also means pushing back against the gates of hell by pulling out of the fire, even with fear (Zech. 3:2; Jude 23), those who do not know the terror of God (2 Cor. 5:11). Augustine teaches us the proper attitude of true Christians: "Our desire ought to be that all may be saved; and hence every person we meet, we will desire to be with us a partaker of peace."[32] Our actions should be in step with our desires. Love for others will move us to warn against hell.

Hell Rounds Out Our Understanding of God

That hell is shocking to our sensitivities—evoking what J. I. Packer labels "traumatic awe"[33]—confirms something about God that we might have missed apart from this dreadful doctrine: God is far less tolerant of evil than we are. Precisely because of our aversion to the notion of sustained condemnation we can better appreciate God's plan to create an eternity in which beauty and peace are inside, and dark arts, sexual perversion, murder, self-worship, and untruth are kept outside (Rev. 22:15). Hell assures us that "we do not worship a cartoon deity. God is not a one-dimensional character out of a summer blockbuster. He's not some petty, insecure despot with lightning bolts who nurses a grudge against the human race. But neither is he a…feel good god eager to cheer on anyone no matter their failings so long as they have a back story."[34] True to His hatred of everything that detracts from human and cosmic flourishing, God will one day make "new heavens and a new earth in which righteousness dwells" (2 Peter 3:13).

---

32. Quoted in Calvin, *Institutes*, 3.23.14.

33. Packer, "The Problem of Eternal Punishment," 21.

34. Kevin DeYoung, "Heaven Is a World of Love," *The Gospel Coalition* (blog), July 15, 2015, https://blogs.thegospelcoalition.org/kevindeyoung/2015/07/15/heaven-is-a-world-of-love/.

Hell Deepens Our Love for Christ

For centuries Christians have confessed the punchy phrase from the Apostles' Creed, "He descended into hell." Christians have not always agreed on what these words mean.[35] But every believer can say that "Christ my Lord, by His inexpressible anguish, pains, and terrors, which He suffered in His soul on the cross and before, has redeemed me from the anguish and torment of hell" (Isa. 53:10; Matt. 27:46).[36] Christ knows hell—by virtue of personal experience—because He endured its horrors instead of those whom He came to save. The doctrine of hell is an unflattering handmaid to the gospel. But as believers shudder at that terrible doctrine, by faith we can sing,

> Bearing shame and scoffing rude,
> In my placed condemned he stood,
> Sealed my pardon with his blood:
> Hallelujah! What a Savior.[37]

---

35. See Daniel R. Hyde, *In Defense of the Descent: A Response to Contemporary Critics* (Grand Rapids: Reformation Heritage Books, 2013).

36. HC 44.

37. *Trinity Psalter Hymnal*, 352.

CHAPTER 10

The New Heavens and Earth

Most of our thoughts about the future are punctuated by question marks. This is true in the very short term, as we wonder what the rest of this week will be like. But when we think about eternity, our questions multiply. For those who treasure Christ's promise—"I go to prepare a place for you.... I will come again and receive you to Myself; that where I am, there you may be also" (John 14:2–3)—one of the biggest questions is, What is heaven like? Even the form of that question implies that we can only think about heaven by analogy. It is *like* a wedding feast (Rev. 19:9), a many-roomed house (John 14:2), a city (Heb. 11:10, 16) with gates of pearls and streets of gold (Rev. 21:21), a country whose hills flow with sweet wine (Amos 9:13).

None of the Bible authors offer anything like a highly descriptive tourist guide to heaven—not even those who had been to heaven and back. After being caught up to paradise Paul could not lawfully express what he had experienced (2 Cor. 12:1–6). To convey his vision of heaven, similes were John's go-to figure of speech; page-for-page the word *like* occurs four times as often in Revelation than in the rest of Scripture. Truly, "eye has not seen, nor ear heard, nor have entered into the heart of man the things which God has prepared for those who love him" (1 Cor. 2:9).[1]

---

1. Paul seems to be alluding to Isaiah 64:4, in the context of which the prophet pleads that God would "rend the heavens" and "come down! That the mountains might shake at Your presence" (v. 1). When Paul insists that "God has

The reward of heaven will be to believers "such a glory as never entered into the heart of man to conceive."[2]

Maybe because heaven seems so unfamiliar to us we struggle to believe it is real. We might not doubt the existence of heaven, but it can still feel less solid, less tangible, than the world we now know. So, how real is heaven? What is it like? And how should the reality of heaven affect us now?

The Reality of Heaven

The biblical descriptions of heaven are indeed heavily metaphorical. This does not, however, argue for heaven's unreality but for its surpassing grandeur. In fact, that the biblical writers could successfully illustrate heaven by way of earthly analogies should suggest to us that the Promised Land is not as unfamiliar as we might suspect. When the ancient Israelites yearned for that "land flowing with milk and honey" (Ex. 3:17) they anticipated something *more* real than that metaphor suggests. They certainly did not imagine a land with milky, sticky rivers, a bizarre ancient-Near-Eastern version of Willy Wonka's chocolate factory. They anticipated a land of bounty, "the most glorious of all lands" (Ezek. 20:6 ESV), and they were not disappointed with what they found (Num. 13:27).

We might also be unnerved because the heaven into which Jesus ascended seems to be dauntingly ethereal, a place humans would find uninhabitable. We might even suspect that "the heaven into which Christ has gone is not a place distinct from earth and hell, but rather just that the heavenly kingdom is present everywhere."[3]

---

revealed them to us through His Spirit" (1 Cor. 2:10), he seems to have in mind the events connected with Christ's first coming. The events following Christ's second coming still remain shrouded in glorious mystery.

2. BC 37.

3. Against which the Bremen Consensus argues, 3:660.

But the Bible speaks of heaven as a definite place, the place where Christ now dwells in real flesh (Acts 1:11). The promise made to the patriarchs, which they did not receive in their day (Heb. 11:13), was a very tangible inheritance of land (Gen. 17:8), or as Paul translates, the *cosmos*, the whole world (Rom. 4:13). God will fulfill that promise to them and their seed in the new heavens and earth (Heb. 11:14–16)—and not by spiritualizing the gift of land into something less substantial.

Dispensational eschatology tends to see the millennium as the time when God fulfills tangible promises of restoration. But what if these promises are fulfilled more richly, not merely during a thousand-year period of partial renewal, but throughout eternity in a renewed heaven and earth?[4] John's Revelation helps us reconcile the apparent discrepancy that Jesus went to heaven by ascending into the air, and God's promise of a highly tangible heaven. In the age to come heaven and earth will not be distinct; heaven will come to earth and "the tabernacle of God" will be "with men, and He will dwell with them" (Rev. 21:3).[5] We should not be surprised if a physical heaven sounds more inviting than a rarefied one. "Our heavenly hope is not only of saved souls but of a saved creation (Rom. 8:19–21).... Whatever the condition of 'the life everlasting,' it is more, certainly not less, than the embodied joy that such imagery suggests. We are creatures of time and space, and we will transcend not our humanity but the bondage of our humanity to the conditions of sin and death."[6]

---

4. See Anthony Hoekema, *The Bible and the Future* (Grand Rapids: Eerdmans, 1994), 275–76.

5. Lest we think that the new heaven and earth must be two distinct places, Vos reminds us that "the OT has no single word for 'universe,' and that the phrase 'heaven and earth' serves to supply the deficiency. The promise of a new heavens and a new earth is therefore the equivalent to a promise of world renewal." James Orr, gen. ed., *The International Standard Bible Encyclopedia* (Grand Rapids: Eerdmans, 1952), s.v. "Heavens, New (and Earth, New)," by Geerhardus Vos.

6. Horton, *Christian Faith*, 988–89. Similarly, Vos says, "The eschatological kingdom differs from the present kingdom largely in the fact that it will receive an

Eternal life will perfectly answer the best longings of God's embodied children. Hoekema writes, "The Bible assures us that God will create a new earth on which we shall live to God's praise in glorified, resurrected bodies. On that new earth, therefore, we hope to spend eternity enjoying its beauties, exploring its resources, and using its treasures to the glory of God."[7] Such is the message of both Testaments of Scripture. In the new heavens and new earth "they shall build houses and inhabit them; they shall plant vineyards and eat their fruit" (Isa. 65:21). God's "elect shall long enjoy the work of their hands. They shall not labor in vain" (vv. 22–23). Animals will populate the age to come though one will no longer prey on another (v. 25).[8] In the age to come, when the kingdom of God is fully bestowed, God's people will eat and drink at Christ's table in His kingdom (Luke 22:17, 29–30; Matt. 8:11).[9] Geerhardus Vos explains that these physical descriptions of the age to come should not "be interpreted allegorically, as if they stood for wholly internal spiritual processes: they evidently point to, or at least include, outward states and activities, of which

---

external, visible embodiment.... It will have its outward form as the doctrine of the resurrection and the regenerated earth plainly show." *Redemptive History*, 54.

7. Hoekema, *Bible and the Future*, 274.

8. The Hungarian Confessio Catholica states, without proof, that while "the material of created things will be renewed and freed from corruption...dumb animals will not be resurrected." Dennison, *Reformed Confessions*, 2:625. Citing Romans 8:22–23 ("the whole creation groans"), Loraine Boettner offers a more balanced conclusion: "As in this present world one generation of plants and animals succeeds another, so in the new earth there will be plant and animal life, no doubt much more luxurious and varied and permanent than here, but...the individual ones that we have known will not be there." *Immortality* (Philadelphia: Presbyterian and Reformed, 1956), 86.

9. Romans 14:17 could seem to suggest that the kingdom is merely spiritual and in no way physical. But Paul is simply making the point that citizenship in God's kingdom does not hinge on how one "[pretends] to champion meat and drink, as though that were essential to God's kingdom." Martin Luther, *Commentary on the Epistle to the Romans* (Grand Rapids: Zondervan, 1954), 188.

our life in the senses offers some analogy."[10] At the same time, if every apocalyptic image of the age to come is not to be taken in a strictly literal manner (e.g., streets of gold), they *are* meant to trigger our imagination to hope for better things.

If this very physical view of heaven somehow seems anticlimactic, we need to ponder God's undiluted approval of His first creation. When God made the heavens and the earth it was undeniably physical, and it was very good (Gen. 1:31). Any vision of an intangible heaven ill-suited to fully embodied humans radically underestimates the vision of Scripture.

The Riches of Heaven

The Bible's promise of eternal life is a promise not only of life without end but also without defect.[11]

Heaven Is a Reversal of the Pain of the Curse

The Bible frequently describes heaven as a place from which everything negative is banished. "And God will wipe away every tear from their eyes; there shall be no more death, nor sorrow, nor crying. There shall be no more pain, for the former things have passed away" (Rev. 21:4). No one in heaven will hunger or thirst (Rev. 7:16) or fear (Rev. 21:8). Earthly relationships in the Lord, now sullied by sin, will be restored.

With the advent of sin people lost closeness with God and with each other, work became painful, and death began to reign (Gen. 3:1–19; Rom. 5:14). The words are hard to read: "The LORD God sent him out of the garden of Eden.... So he drove out the man" so he could not eat of the tree of life and live forever (Gen. 3:22–24). In the new heaven and earth Christ grants His friends

---

10. Vos, *Redemptive History*, 54. Elsewhere Vos explains that regarding the creation of the new heavens and earth, Scripture anticipates "*a restoration of the primeval harmony* on a higher plane such as precludes all further disturbance" (emphasis added). Orr, "Heavens, New."

11. Vos, *Redemptive History*, 54.

"to eat from the tree of life, which is in the midst of the Paradise of God" (Rev. 2:7).

Christ's overthrow of sin at the last day will destroy its negative consequences so familiar to us. In heaven, "they shall be fully and forever freed from all sin and misery."[12] Even things we now find tiresome, like work, will become a great delight. If you could imagine without limits and build without frustration or disappointment, if your body never ached and your plans never failed, would not work be enjoyable? When God renews the world, which was created for humans' sake, it "shall at length be renewed and be clad with another hue, much more pleasant and beautiful."[13] Never again will God's people encounter an unclean thing (Rev. 21:27). When God finishes reversing the curse in the new heavens and earth (Rev. 22:3) He will restore everything that was lost. In those days will the former troubles be forgotten for God's children (Isa. 65:16).

Heaven Is a Realization of Fellowship with God
We who are but "a particle of [God's] creation" long, more than anything, to know God and be known by Him.[14] Believers gain great comfort from their present status as children of God. But our present relationship with our Father is strained by our misunderstanding of His purposes and disobedience of His will. The friendship with God we now experience in part, we will gain fully in heaven (1 Cor. 13:12). John sees it this way: "Beloved, now we are children of God; and it has not yet been revealed what we shall be, but we know that when He is revealed, we shall be like Him, for we shall see Him as He is" (1 John 3:2). The elect shall enjoy eternity "in the company of innumerable saints and holy angels, but especially in the immediate vision and fruition of God the Father, of our Lord Jesus Christ, and of the Holy Spirit, to

---

12. WLC 90.
13. Anglican Catechism (1553), 2:29.
14. Augustine, *The Confessions* (New York: E. P. Dutton, 1949), 1.

all eternity." The communion which "the members of the invisible church shall enjoy with Christ in glory" shall be "perfect and full."[15] Heaven, as one of our young daughters once suggested, is the place where God keeps His promises, and the essence of His promise is perfect friendship.

Heaven Is a Realm of Worship

One heavenly scene that John repeatedly records is the exuberant worship of the redeemed (Rev. 4:8–11; 5:9–14; 7:10–12; 11:16–19; 15:3–4; 16:5–7). If the everlasting worship of God does not seem altogether inviting now—imagine a Sunday service that never ended—it is because our present worship is disrupted by sin and weakness. Now we worship God with mixed desires; then our love for God will be perfected (Jude 21). Now we worship in bodies given to fatigue and distraction; then our bodies will be incorruptible (1 Cor. 15:42). Now we worship in churches populated by people who hurt and misjudge each other; then we will truly be a holy family, finally able to consistently love our neighbor as ourselves. As we worship God now, He sometimes seems distant (Ps. 10:1). Then He will always be present (Ps. 16:11), and we will glorify and enjoy Him as never before.

Heaven Will Host a Renewed Humanity

In heaven believers shall be "filled with inconceivable joys, made perfectly holy and happy both in body and soul."[16] And not simply in the abstract but in pursuit of the best thoughts and activities that currently mark our humanity. God made people to be culture-makers (Gen. 2:5; 4:19–22). Should we suspect that His vision for creaturely creativity will diminish in the age to come? Anthony Hoekema reflects the sentiments of Hendrikus Berkhof and Abraham Kuyper in suggesting that "the unique contributions

15. WLC 90.
16. WLC 90.

of each nation to the life of the present earth will enrich the life of the new earth" and that the redeemed will "inherit the best products of culture and art which this earth has produced."[17] In his glorious vision of the new heaven and earth John previewed the nations and kings of the earth bringing their glory and honor, cultural products in the form of gifts and sacrifices, into the holy city (Rev. 21:24–27).[18]

Heaven is an inestimably great reward (1 Peter 5:4) tailor-made for God's beloved people which we should pursue at all cost (Matt. 13:45–46). That some will find heaven to be a greater reward than others (Luke 19:15–19) should not bother us. If even now we are encouraged to "rejoice with those who rejoice" (Rom. 12:15) we can expect the entire category of unfairness to vanish with this old earth.

The Response to Heaven

God breathes into our hearts the hope of heaven to help us on our journey to that great city.

Heaven Excites Us to Practice God's Will

Jesus taught His disciples to pray to our Father, "Your kingdom come. Your will be done on earth as it is in heaven" (Matt. 6:10). With this prayer we recognize that only God can make us more heavenly, while fervently committing to put into practice a divine ethic (see Phil. 2:12–13). We should pray and strive "that we all may live on earth as in heaven, with all joy and gladness, according to his divine will."[19] As the new heaven and earth are

---

17. Hoekema, *Bible and the Future*, 286.

18. Dennis Johnson comments that the nations will bring their "wealth" into the city though not for the purpose of consumption but as "gifts and sacrifices of the earthly sanctuary, to be offered to the divine King enthroned on it." *Triumph of the Lamb: A Commentary on Revelation* (Phillipsburg, N.J.: P&R, 2001), 318–19.

19. Large Emden Catechism, 1:632. "Heaven is in the consciousness of Jesus the goal towards which every aspiration of the disciple in the kingdom ought to tend" (see Matt. 6:19–21). Vos, *Redemptive History*, 306.

"an eternal, happy Sabbath from all deadly works"[20] we ought to begin this rest here and now.[21]

Heaven Trains Us to Respect God's Earth

Strangely, some people who seem the least interested in a creator are the most zealous for creation, while those with a rich theology of divine creation and (at least the raw materials for) a theology of the restoration of the cosmos sometimes seem the least interested in ecological stewardship.

This should not be. As Horton writes, "If our goal is to be liberated *from* creation rather than the liberation *of* creation, we will understandably display little concern for the world that God has made. If, however, we are looking forward to 'the restoration of all things' (Acts 3:21) and the participation of the whole creation in our redemption (Rom. 8:18–21), then our actions here and now pertain to the same world that will one day be finally and fully renewed."[22] Humans are the proper image of God. But the rest of God's creation—like that which He purified with the great flood—is good and should be treasured by believers because it "leads us to contemplate the invisible things of God, namely, His eternal power and divinity, as the apostle Paul saith (Rom. 1:20)."[23] Calvin is right, "Wherever you turn your eyes, there is no portion of the world, however minute, that does not exhibit at least some sparks of beauty" and overwhelm us by "the immense weight of glory."[24] How can this reality not mightily impact Christian ecology?

---

20. Large Emden Catechism, 1:598.

21. HC 103.

22. Horton, *Christian Faith*, 989–90.

23. BC 2.

24. Calvin, *Institutes*, 1.5.1. Thanks to John Jeffery for drawing my attention to this quote and to the many places in the *Institutes* where Calvin speaks of the majestic "theater" of creation (e.g., 1.5.8; 1.6.2; 1.14.20; 2.6.1).

Heaven Encourages Us to Pursue Deep Fellowship

Heaven will be quintessentially relational. Those concerned that marriages will cease in glory (Mark 12:25) will be overjoyed to find that the most transferable traits of marriage will then be shared by heaven's entire population. There is no doubt that we will deeply recognize (to put it too mildly) our redeemed friends as well as the vast host of God's people.[25] Fittingly, the Somerset Confession (1656) follows its article on heaven by insisting that "it is both the duty and privilege of the church of Christ (till His coming again)…to enjoy, prize, and press after, fellowship through and in the Spirit with the Lord, and each with the other (Acts 2:42; 1 Cor. 11:26; Eph. 2:21–22; 4:3–6; 1 Cor. 12:13; Eph. 3:9; Col. 2:2)."[26] One of the best ways to show an interest in heaven is to begin to live in harmonious love with others, especially with other believers.

Heaven Helps Us to Be Patient in Tribulation

A theology of "suffering which says nothing of heaven, is leaving out almost the whole of one side of the account."[27] Randy Alcorn reflects on Lewis's thought: "Present sufferings *must* be seen in light of the promise of eternal happiness in God. The scales can't be balanced in this life alone." But as Paul says, "Our light affliction…is working for us a far more exceeding and eternal weight of glory" (2 Cor. 4:17). Again, Alcorn says, "It's not that temporary suffering is so *small*; it's that eternal glory is so *huge*."[28] Believers, even in the midst of the greatest tribulation, can confidently expect God to wipe away their tears and remove their

---

25. Though the disciples clearly felt out of place by the meeting, they certainly knew Moses and Elijah, who appeared with Jesus on the Mount of Transfiguration, having been dead for hundreds of years (Matt. 17:3).

26. Somerset Confession, 4:455.

27. C. S. Lewis, *The Problem of Pain*, in *The C. S. Lewis Signature Classics* (New York: HarperCollins, 2017), 638.

28. Randy Alcorn, "C. S. Lewis on Heaven and the New Earth: God's Eternal Remedy to the Problem of Evil and Suffering," *Desiring God* (blog),

rebuke (Isa. 25:8; Rev. 7:14–17). We can better endure reproach when our hearts are set on a greater reward (Heb. 11:26; 12:2).

Heaven Helps Us to Long for God

Wilhelmus à Brakel urges believers to "focus continually upon the glory of this inheritance, and by faith traverse heaven" by using John's Revelation as a glimpse into their future.[29] In Scripture, wrote Richard Baxter, "heaven is set open, as it were, to our daily view" for our encouragement, that we might long for the city of God (Heb. 11:10) and enter therein.[30] This longing for glory does not distract us from godliness but infuses in us the kind of hopeful disposition necessary to follow God and rejoice in the hope of His glory (Rom. 5:2).

One of the most beautiful images of heaven is also the simplest and most familiar to us. Heaven is home. As a pastor, I commonly hear death-bed-ridden believers say, "I want to go home." Heaven-as-home is a concept many believers have learned from the Psalms. My grandfather chose Psalm 84 as his funeral text. After a ninety-seven-year pilgrimage he could say with the writer: "My soul longs, yes, even faints for the courts of the LORD" (v. 2). He had come to believe that a day in God's courts is better than a thousand elsewhere (v. 10). But he was not enamored with the beauty of God's tabernacle (v. 1) because of its architecture. His deepest longing was to be with God. "My heart and my flesh cry out for the living God" (v. 2). A home is a place where one feels native, where fears of exclusion melt away. To make his point, the psalmist speaks of a sparrow finding a home for her young. Like

Sept. 28, 2013, http://www.desiringgod.org/messages/c-s-lewis-on-heaven-and-the-new-earth-god-s-eternal-remedy-to-the-problem-of-evil-and-suffering.

29. Wilhelmus à Brakel, *The Christian's Reasonable Service* (Grand Rapids: Reformation Heritage Books, 1995), 4:368. The closing section of Brakel's dogmatics unravels the false notion that heavenly-mindedness results in spiritual laziness (see especially 367–70).

30. Richard Baxter, *The Saints' Everlasting Rest* (Fearn, Ross-Shire, Scotland: Christian Focus, 1998), 656.

that nest—built to fit around her young—believers will be able to say without hesitation, "The Lord of Hosts is nigh, our father's God Most High is our strong habitation."[31]

Have you ever been on vacation and found yourself eager to get home? Similarly, a longing for heaven can speed and strengthen us on our way to God.

---

31. Metrical version of Psalm 46. *Trinity Psalter Hymnal*, 46C.

APPLIED ESCHATOLOGY

CHAPTER 11

The End Times and the Kingdom of God

"The time is fulfilled, and the kingdom of God is at hand. Repent, and believe in the gospel" (Mark 1:15). In Jesus's first public ministry speech He powerfully linked the kingdom of God and the last things. The doctrine of eschatology is like the final chapters of the unfolding story of the constitution of God's kingdom.[1] From the beginning of creation, God has been working out a majestic plan not merely to save souls (certainly not apart from bodies), but to display His glorious reign over everything. The doctrines of the end times and the kingdom of God come together to help us see how God has been establishing His reign and how He will perfect it.

And this is very important. Especially when set within the broader context of *kingdom*, eschatology has the potential to unlock a largeness of the Christian faith that is often unrealized. Too often Christianity is seen simply as a means of escaping hell, a sort of eternal-fire insurance policy. With such a view, virtually nothing else matters except "going to heaven when I die." Tragically, those who adopt such a religion close their eyes to much of the beauty of the new world God is opening up to His people now. They risk becoming like the foolish virgins of Jesus's parable who desired to enter the wedding banquet but slept during

---

1. Herman Ridderbos, *The Coming of the Kingdom* (Philadelphia: Presbyterian and Reformed, 1962), 24–25.

the days of preparation (Matt. 25:1–13). A true interest in the end of God's work demands an interest in His work now. The biblical theme of kingdom draws together the two epochs of God's work.

Understanding God's Eschatological Kingdom

Geerhardus Vos is right: "The conception of the kingdom of God is one of those conceptions which, owing to our very familiarity with them and their highly generalizing character, have become almost mere conventional signs."[2] The Bible student who fails to appreciate the kingdom is like a fish that fails to give much thought to water. But judging from the way Jesus, as well as His immediate predecessors and students, echoed the Old Testament concept of the kingdom of God, it is clearly a dominant thread in the story of redemptive history.

The Story of the Kingdom

Like every good story, the biblical narrative of the kingdom has a beginning, a middle, and an end. First, God promised a coming kingdom. From its first breath creation belonged to the King of Glory. "The earth is the LORD's, and all its fullness, the world and those who dwell therein. For He has founded it upon the seas, and established it upon the waters" (Ps. 24:1–2). For reasons known only to Himself (though ultimately resulting in the magnification of His glory), He allowed sin to poison this world. Even after the revolt of some of His angels (Rev. 12:9; Isa. 14:12–15) and people, God did not relinquish His kingdom. Instead, as the great King, He promised violent judgment against implacable rebels and established a gracious covenant with all those who would live under His rule (Gen. 3:14–15). After shepherding a modest band of God-followers through the tumultuous early generations of this earth, God promised to make Abraham a great nation (Gen. 12:2), later known as Israel, through whom "all the families of the earth shall be blessed" (v. 3). From the start God's

---

2. Vos, *Redemptive History*, 310.

salvation of Israel was always aimed at a grander work of redemption. God's Old Testament kingdom-building is seen most plainly in the era of the kings. God promised His servant David an eternal kingdom (2 Sam. 7:16), though after just a few generations of heirs it became clear that "the perfect realization of the kingdom could not be a matter of the present, but would have to belong to the future." The prophets, especially Daniel, declared that God's future kingdom would "overthrow and replace the great world monarchies."[3] This overthrow began with Christ's advent and the coming-of-age of the church (Gal. 4:1–5).

Second, God inaugurated the kingdom. When the angel Gabriel (Luke 1:33), John the Baptist (Matt. 3:2), Jesus (Mark 1:14–15), the twelve disciples (Luke 9:1–6), and Paul (Acts 14:22) preached a message of the kingdom of God they were building on Old Testament expectations that the coming of Messiah would set in motion events that would result in a mighty, unending kingdom. At Christ's incarnation a stone, "cut…without hands," had begun rolling down a mountain and could not be stopped. It would "break in pieces and consume" all other kingdoms (Dan. 2:44–45). At His coming, Christ began to beat back the devil's stolen gains. After centuries of waiting it was finally evident that one day the shout of victory would burst forth: "The kingdoms of this world have become the kingdoms of our Lord and of His Christ, and He shall reign forever and ever!" (Rev. 11:15). In the coming of Christ, "the powers which will revolutionize heaven and earth are already in motion."[4] Third, God will one day consummate the kingdom. The kingdom will fully come when God dismisses the wicked and establishes his throne in righteousness (Prov. 25:5). He will be all in all when every enemy is placed under His feet (1 Cor. 15:24–28) and every friend is safely gathered into His country. After the final judgment all the redeemed will praise

---

3. Vos, *Redemptive History*, 304–5.
4. Vos, *Redemptive History*, 312.

God saying, "You have taken Your great power and reigned" and destroyed "those who destroy the earth" (Rev. 11:17–18).

The Nature of God's Kingdom

The biblical concept of God's kingdom conveys both His reign and the realm of His reign. During this age, God exercises His reign while preparing to unveil the realm of His kingdom in the new heaven and new earth. Presently, God is establishing His kingdom spiritually through the conquest of individual hearts and lives. He is forming a community of kingdom citizens who live under His gracious reign. But at the last day He will decisively perfect the kingdom by creating a new heaven and new earth as the dwelling place of unblemished righteousness. On that day God's spiritual kingdom will be realized in an "external, visible sphere."[5] At present, righteousness inhabits Zion—His commu- nity of redeemed people—(Isa. 33:5); one day it will inhabit the new heaven and new earth (2 Peter 3:13). The kingdom is not something we can make; we can only receive it. But "since we are receiving a kingdom which cannot be shaken, let us have grace, by which we may serve God acceptably with reverence and godly fear" (Heb. 12:28).

Living in God's Eschatological Kingdom

So why is it important to think about the end times in terms of God's present and future kingdom? Simply put, a kingdom escha- tology gives us hope to live out our challenging callings in this age as we prepare to inherit the earth (Ps. 25:13; Matt. 5:5).

The Believer's Kingdom Hope

God's children are part of a movement far grander than they often realize. Believers "upon whom the ends of the ages have come" live in an extraordinarily privileged day (1 Cor. 10:11). Jesus didn't exaggerate when He said, "He who is least in the

---

5. Vos, *Redemptive History*, 310.

kingdom of heaven is greater" than John the Baptist (Matt. 11:11).
The last days are good days in which to know the Lord! It is true,
as the apostles wrote, "in the last days perilous times will come"
(2 Tim. 3:1; cf. 1 Tim. 4:1; 2 Peter 3:3; 1 John 2:18; Jude 17–18).
But whereas these challenges have always existed (1 Cor. 10:13),
end-times believers have powerful new reasons to be hopeful.

The triune God is actively perfecting an unshakable kingdom (Heb. 12:28). The Father reigns in majesty. In Psalm 47
the writers blend images of a future glory—"He will subdue the
peoples under us, and the nations under our feet" (v. 3)—with
images of His present rule—"God reigns over the nations; God
sits on His holy throne…. He is greatly exalted" (vv. 8–9). Right
now God laughs at those who plot His overthrow (Ps. 2:4; 37:13).
The Son orchestrates the movements of human history. Christ
alone is "worthy to take the scroll" upon which is written everything that shall come to pass, "and to open its seals" (Rev. 5:9).[6]
Insofar as Christ's reign presently feels unimpressive and insignificant, by faith we can confidently expect King Jesus to one day
make everything right (Heb. 2:8–9). The Spirit is building the
kingdom in and around us. "Jesus ascribes all the power involved
in the establishment of the kingdom to the Holy Spirit as its
source."[7] The Spirit supernaturally begets sons of the kingdom
(John 3:5). By the Spirit, Christ threw out demons, signifying
that the "kingdom of God has come upon you" (Matt. 12:28).
Paul says that the kingdom of God is "peace and joy in the Holy
Spirit" (Rom. 14:17) that we can enjoy even when we make sacrifices for the sake of others.

---

6. This sealed scroll is a crisis. "The things written in the scroll 'must take
place' because they constitute God's plan for his history, culminating in the vindication of his servants and the unchallenged establishment of his dominion on
earth, as it is in heaven." Johnson, *Triumph of the Lamb*, 105. Christ alone is able to
open the scroll because "the future and final victory of Messiah is but an extension of the rule he now enjoys by virtue of the victory already won." George Eldon
Ladd, *A Commentary on the Revelation of John* (Grand Rapids: Eerdmans, 1972), 85.

7. Vos, *Redemptive History*, 313.

Geerhardus Vos explains that the kingdom of God "is the sphere in which God as the Supreme Ruler and Judge carries out His holy will in righteousness and judgment."[8] God is presently working His righteous will in this world. He is presently restraining and punishing evil (Job 1:12; 2:6) and rewarding righteousness (Mark 10:29–31). He is breathing new life into people, making them able to reflect His quest for true shalom. The kingdom began small—like a mustard seed (Mark 4:30–32)—but God is patiently raising up a kingdom of priests, holy to the Lord.

God offers the gift of His church as both the fruit and a foretaste of God's perfected kingdom. When the Bible speaks of God's kingdom, it sometimes describes a structured organization, typified by the Old Testament theocracy and only fully realized in the age to come (see Acts 1:6). At other times the kingdom of God is described in more organic terms. Jesus said, "The kingdom of God is within you" (Luke 17:21) like a seed of God-likeness.[9] Bridging these two concepts is the church, a unique "phase in the development of the kingdom of God."[10] The church is both a structural organization that has grown out of the obsolete Old Testament theocracy and a spiritual organism made up of all those who are panting for God and the completion of the kingdom.[11] True churches of Christ are far more than a convenient social group or spiritual drive-through. Instead, they preview the kingdom in which believers rest together in God's grace and presence and also hear His loving voice. In the church we can help bear one another's burdens until burdens are no more[12] and weep

---

8. Vos, *Redemptive History*, 313.

9. For a study of Jesus's parables in which He describes the kingdom in organic, internally spiritual terms, see my *Bible Studies on Mark* (Grand Rapids: Reformed Fellowship, 2016), 54–57.

10. Vos, *Redemption History*, 316.

11. On the distinction between the visible church as organism and organization, see Louis Berkhof, *Systematic Theology* (Grand Rapids: Eerdmans, 1941), 567.

12. For a brief, practical encouragement in burden bearing, see John McArthur, "Bearing One Another's Burdens," *Ligonier Ministries* (blog), Jan. 1, 2010,

with those who weep (Rom. 12:15) until the time for weeping and mourning has turned to laughing and dancing (Eccl. 3:4). The church is not heaven, but it is without parallel in its ability to put the taste of heaven in our mouths.[13]

The Believer's Kingdom Responsibility
It is only with a vibrant kingdom hope that God's people will be energized to pursue the robust life of purity and holiness required of kingdom citizens (1 John 3:3; Heb. 12:15). "Genuine hope comes to visibility in action."[14] George Eldon Ladd ties together God's giving of a kingdom with believers' assumption of kingdom responsibilities: "God's people are a kingdom not merely because they are the people over whom God reigns, but because they are to participate in the messianic reign of Christ."[15] Like yeast in dough, "the reign of God, introduced into human hearts and lives *from without*, once having entered, exerts a wholesome, penetrating, and transforming influence *within and from within outward*, upon hearts and lives."[16] When God captures our hearts we seek first His kingdom and righteousness, unwilling to be distracted by worldly allurements (Matt. 6:33–34). Thus, "the striving after righteousness is made the absolutely supreme concern of the disciple. He must hunger and thirst after it, endure persecution for its sake, sacrifice it for all other things."[17] And believers are moti-

https://www.ligonier.org/learn/articles/bearing-one-anothers-burdens/.

13. "Church is the core element in the strategy of the Holy Spirit for providing human witness and physical presence to the Jesus-inaugurated kingdom of God in this world. It is not that kingdom complete, but it is a witness to that kingdom." Eugene Peterson, *Practice Resurrection: A Conversation on Growing Up in Christ* (Grand Rapids: Eerdmans, 2010), 12.

14. Richard C. Oudersluys, "The Parable of the Sheep and Goats (Matthew 25:31–46): Eschatology and Mission, Then and Now," *Reformed Review* 26 (Spring 1973): 158.

15. Ladd, *A Commentary on the Revelation*, 27.

16. William Hendriksen, *The Gospel of Luke*, New Testament Commentary (Grand Rapids: Baker, 1978), 704.

17. Vos, *Redemptive History*, 313.

vated to do so because of the great reward of the kingdom; not a truncated reward of going to heaven upon death, but the promise of being raised up from the "beggarly elements" (Gal. 4:9) to a holistic new life in the kingdom. With this restored vision for the good life,

> The believer's purpose is…everywhere to bring every thought of whatever kind into submission to, and therefore harmony with, the mind and will of Christ (see II Cor. 10:5)…. Therefore Christ's true follower actively promotes such cases as the abolition of slavery, the restoration of women's rights, the alleviation of poverty, the repatriation, if practicable, of the displaced…the education of the illiterate, the reorientation of fine arts along Christian lines, etc. He promotes honesty among those who govern and those who are governed, as well as in business, industry, and commerce.[18]

It is not enough for the church to wait for God to make everything right, to make straight every crooked thing and to level every rough place (Luke 3:5). God's people will begin to put into practice now the social righteousness that will permeate the new heaven and new earth. The true pursuit of justice must not be relegated to social-gospel congregations nor should justice-seeking churches become political animals.[19] There is a way to echo God's concern for the poor, the unborn, the widow, the wanderer, without forsaking our highest calling to direct sinners to find their hope in Christ. Throughout His ministry, by word and deed, Jesus made it clear that "the poor, the sinner,

---

18. Hendriksen, *Gospel of Luke*, 704. Hendriksen adds, "The difference between 'the social gospel' and the teaching of this parable is that the former focuses its attention solely on society as a whole, neglecting the needs of individual hearts and lives, while the latter, by first of all radically changing hearts and lives, works from within outward, thus creating better conditions all around," 712.

19. In fact, to do so is to revert to the error of many Jewish people in Jesus's day who dreamed of a merely political kingdom. See Vos, *Redemptive History*, 310.

the sick, the beggar, and the religious outcast are welcome in the kingdom."[20] Are they welcome into our lives? Your church doesn't have an "Outcasts Not Welcome Here" sign on its door. But do you pursue the poor like Jesus did? He traveled to their ghettos and countrysides, preaching the gospel as a sign of the in-breaking kingdom (Luke 7:22) that explicitly included them (Matt. 11:2–6; Luke 4:18–19). A rich eschatology, with a firm commitment to invest now in the age to come, will lead us to share with Jesus a loose hold on our resources (Luke 16:1–13). With keen intentionality Paul referenced the Ephesian Christians' future inheritance of glory to stimulate their present generosity (Acts 20:32–35).

For members of God's eschatological kingdom, godliness matters because everything matters. During a particularly confusing time of life, Sharon Creech's fictional protagonist in *Walk Two Moons* pondered this proverb: "In the course of a lifetime what does it matter?" If humans are merely infinitesimal specks of dust being poured into the black hole of eternity, then everything is meaningless. But if the God of heaven is drawing us into a kingdom that will never be destroyed (Dan. 2:44), then everything matters. The Christian message—a story of the ultimate establishment of God's kingdom through the restoring power of the gospel—undermines competing narratives that degrade human dignity. It is difficult to imagine a message more relevant for a meaning-starved culture that has become dubious of the old narrative of divine salvation.

God's people battle against the devil, the flesh, and the world, all of which are violently raging against God's promise of a final judgment. Through the kingdom motif, what God said to King Asa, He says to all believers: "But you, be strong and do not let your hands be weak, for your work shall be rewarded" (2 Chron. 15:7).

---

20. Michael Goheen, *A Light to the Nations: The Missional Church and the Biblical Story* (Grand Rapids: Baker Academic, 2011), 93.

CHAPTER 12

The End Times and the Mission of the Church

Christian eschatology is a theology of waiting. The King has traveled to a far country and has been a long time in returning (Matt. 25:14, 19). In His absence the saints who keep watch cry (though not without hope), "how long [until] the night of weeping shall be the morn of song?"[1] God's people cry, "Come, Lord Jesus!" (Rev. 22:20). Why doesn't He?

The Bible's answer: God is patiently waiting and working for the gospel to be declared to every creature (Mark 16:15; cf. Matt. 24:14) so that the perishing will be saved (2 Peter 3:9) and the full number of the elect gathered in (Mark 13:27). Christ has not yet finished His mission to seek and save the lost (Luke 19:10), so He refrains from shaking the heavens and the earth by His return (Heb. 12:26–27). *Missions* is the clear answer to the eschatological question, Why hasn't Jesus returned?

Has the church missed the connection between Jesus's delay, God's plan to gather the nations, and our call to missions? One might expect that God's priority of rescue would be mirrored by His redeemed people, yet church "ministry" often amounts to a colossal emphasis on maintenance. Why is it that the average American Christian gives only one penny a day to global missions?[2] Why does the money many churches allocate for local

---

1. *Trinity Psalter Hymnal*, 404.
2. K. P. Yohannan, *Revolution in World Missions* (Carrollton, Tex.: GFA Books, 2002), 142.

evangelism amount to such a slim percentage of the total budget? Is it fair to say that the mission in many churches revolves around holding worship services for believers and teaching believers and their children how to be more faithful? If so, we need a bolder message of the church's radically outward-focused mission.

God's plan for the renewal of all things and the reconstitution of a holy humanity has always been to gather a people who would begin enjoying heaven on earth in a renewed relationship with God, *in order* to be a light to the nations. So, how can a biblical eschatology paradigmatically shift how we view missions? How can a rich doctrine of the last things reorient our understanding of missions from tangent to priority?

Developing an Eschatological Missiology

To grasp the church's missionary calling we have to understand its relationship to Old Testament Israel. William Manson prefaces his entire presentation of "The Biblical Doctrine of Mission" by saying, "In the Bible the conception of the Church's universal mission is bound up, first and last, with the thought of the church being 'the Israel of God.'"[3] Paul can sign off his letter to the churches of Galatia with a benediction to "the Israel of God" (Gal. 6:16) because "the church [is] the true spiritual Israel."[4] In Christ, "all believers…are the true circumcision who worship God in spirit and glory in Christ Jesus (Phil. 3:3)."[5] The church has not replaced Israel but, under the influence of the Spirit's outpouring,

3. William Manson, "The Biblical Doctrine of Mission," *International Review of Mission* 42, no. 167 (July 1953): 257.

4. George Eldon Ladd, *A Theology of the New Testament* (Grand Rapids: Eerdmans, 1974), 539. That Paul would identify the church with an Old Testament term is consistent with his earlier use of a phrase like "the Jerusalem above" to identify the children of promise of both Testaments (Gal. 4:21–31).

5. Ladd, *Theology of the New Testament*, 538.

has become what God always intended Israel to be: a people brought near to Him through the mediation of the Messiah.[6]

Why is this point important? Because God's church today is called to fulfill the mandate that He first gave to Israel.

Israel Was Called to Be a Light to the Nations

Contrary to appearances Israel was meant to be God's mission agency. Missions was not to be an incidental activity for Israel or an elective to be pursued when resources and leisure time permitted. Rather, Israel was bound by covenant to the one true God whose eternal mission was to gather a mighty nation of worshipers.[7] Before Israel entered Egypt, God promised to make Abraham "a great nation" so that in him "all the families of the earth shall be blessed" (Gen. 12:2–3). In striking this promise to Abraham, God reinforced His original intent that His people would be fruitful and multiply within His sphere of blessing (Gen. 1:28). When Israel emerged from Egypt—no longer as a single family of seventy persons (Gen. 46:27) but a mighty nation of millions—the Lord reminded her that she had been birthed through deliverance from chattel slavery (Ex. 20:2). This redeemed identity was to guide the people of Israel forever, prompting them to show special concern to the lost because they knew the bitterness of enslavement and the joy of deliverance (Deut. 10:19).

To see God's people merely as a rescued community is to sharply diminish God's purpose; Israel was also to be a *rescuing*

---

6. Louis Berkhof succinctly explains the historic Reformed understanding not of a "replacement theology" but that "in essence Israel constituted the Church of God in the Old Testament, though its external institution differed vastly from that of the Church in the New Testament." *Systematic Theology*, 571–72. Missiologist Michael Goheen applies this ecclesiological understanding to the work of Jesus and the missional calling of the church: "It is not that the church is displacing Israel. Jesus is not founding a brand-new community. Rather, Israel itself is being purified and reconstituted." *Light to the Nations*, 84.

7. For a good introduction to the eternal covenant of redemption, see Brown and Keele, *Sacred Bond*, 25–41.

community. "It is too small a thing that You should be My Servant to raise up the tribes of Jacob, and to restore the preserved ones of Israel; I will also give You as a light to the Gentiles, that You should be My salvation to the ends of the earth" (Isa. 49:6).[8] As a portrait of God's grace Israel was to magnetically draw in outsiders jealous of her righteousness (Isa. 60:2–3). In this sense, her mission was passive. As Manson says, "Israel's Mission [was] to be achieved by her purification under the hand of God and her glorification through His grace."[9] But she was also to be the voice of God to the nations. Most memorably God raised up prophets like Jonah and Ezekiel to preach the gospel to Gentiles. But even in their worship God's people were to invite the whole earth to "make a joyful shout to God" (Ps. 66:1). They were to welcome outsiders to "come and see the works of God" (v. 5). God's rule was lauded as good news to all people (Ps. 97:1).

For the Israel of God "to be a light to the nations, two things must take place: first, Israel must be *gathered* into a community, and then its people must be *renewed* to live in obedience" to God's will.[10]

The Church Is Called to Be a Light to the Nations

Israel's role as a light to the nations is predictive and prophetic. With the coming of the fullness of time, Christ has come as a greater Moses (Heb. 3:1–6) to accomplish a greater Passover and a more universal exodus of slaves from the kingdom of darkness. It is not until the coming of Christ, the light of the world, that "all peoples" are finally introduced to God's salvation, "a light to bring revelation to the Gentiles, and the glory of Your people Israel" (Luke 2:31–32). At the beginning of the last days Christ

---

8. This prophecy is an example of prophetic foreshortening where the calling of Israel typified the calling of Jesus. On this prophetic phenomena, see Anthony Hoekema, *The Bible and the Future* (Grand Rapids: Eerdmans, 1979), 148–49.

9. Manson, "Biblical Doctrine of Mission," 261.

10. Goheen, *Light to the Nations*, 81.

promised to pour out His spirit to help God's people witness to the coming of the kingdom (Acts 1:8) and keep the light of Christ shining before the nations (Matt. 5:14).

In God's great work of salvation, this present age "is an era of gathering and mission."[11] As the church in these last days learns from Israel's example (1 Cor. 10:11) believers will not view themselves simply as within the walls of safety but as gatherers of those without. In fact, "those who most eagerly look for the return of their Lord will be the most earnest in pressing for the accomplishment" of the Great Commission, "believing that there is something more than youthful fancy in the familiar watch-word of a great missionary movement: 'The Evangelization of the world in this generation.'"[12]

Applying an Eschatological Missiology

It is easy to criticize Israel's failure to care about the nations; it is much harder to see that the church can easily slump toward a self-focused eschatology. How can the church apply a biblical end-times theology of mission to be a more faithful witness? The encouragements that follow are far from exhaustive, but they might help point us in the right direction.

Missional Christians Will Pursue God with Abounding Hope

In a dreary, sin-infected world an eschatology of hope promotes an interest in the gospel (1 Peter 3:16). The church is "a colony of heaven in the country of death";[13] her hopeful pursuit of God makes His story believable and desirable. No one will care about our Christianity if they can't see how it makes our lives more joyful and hopeful. Goheen writes, "The lives of Jesus's followers are

---

11. Goheen, *Light to the Nations*, 80.

12. Charles Erdman, *The Return of Christ* (New York: George H. Doran, 1922), 101–2.

13. Peterson, *Practice Resurrection*, 12.

to be signs of the kingdom, of the healing and liberating power of God breaking through into history."[14]

Missional Christians Will Harmonize Election, Eschatology, and Mission

On the last day God will gather His elect from the earth (Mark 13:27); the Lord knows who are His (2 Tim. 2:19) and He will not fail to save any of those whom He had chosen from before the foundation of the world (Eph. 1:4). If we think these indisputable facts provide a disincentive for the active work of missions, we completely miss God's point. During a particularly discouraging ministry phase Christ encouraged Paul to persevere in the work of gospel ministry *on the ground of divine election* (Acts 18:9–10). Rather than negating the importance of missions, election encourages us that God's unfinished work of people-gathering will bear fruit and that He delights to use us as instruments of salvation.[15]

Missional Christians Will Treasure a Rich and Inviting View of Heaven

With a vague or ethereal concept of heaven we have nothing very tangible to invite people *to*; our "evangelistic" message gets reduced to "turn or burn," and heaven becomes merely the default prize for avoiding the terrors of hell. Central to the message of the church during the last days must be an invitation to the hungry, tired, ashamed, and empty to become new creations and begin dining with Christ while anticipating breaking out of the cocoon of corruptible humanity at Christ's second coming. Heaven is the social event of forever; why shouldn't *that* be integral to our retelling of the good news?

---

14. Goheen, *Light to the Nations*, 88.

15. For an extended engagement on the themes of evangelism and election, see J. I. Packer, *Evangelism and the Sovereignty of God* (Downers Grove, Ill.: Inter-Varsity Press, 1961).

Missional Christians Will Retain the Doctrine of Hell

While preaching on hell, Spurgeon said, "What is written in the Bible must be preached, whether it be gloomy or cheerful."[16] Hell is gloomy. It has always been an awkward topic, sometimes even embarrassing. But Spurgeon also said, "If sinners will be damned, at least let them leap to hell over our bodies; and if they will perish, let them perish with our arms about their knees, imploring them to stay, and not madly to destroy themselves. If hell must be filled, at least let it be filled in the teeth of our exertions, and let not one go there unwarned and unprayed for."[17] A biblical eschatology confronts us with the tragic reality: hell will be populated.

But a biblical eschatology also radically affects the message of the missional church. Our message is not simply a rescue plan for individuals. It is the much bolder message that the kingdom has arrived and that it is time for everyone to participate in God's work of making all things new. Jesus's resurrection assures us that "God's new creation has begun—and we, his followers, have a job to do!"[18] Jesus sent out His disciples the way a conquering king sends out envoys at the head of an army (Luke 9:1–6). He does not (just) plead for converts; He graciously invites a conquered people to join Him in the empire He's building.[19] At the same time, those who eschew God's kingdom must hear that they risk losing the invitation of peace with God (Matt. 10:13; Rom. 5:1), access to heaven, hope in His glory, transformation through trials, and a reformed character (vv. 2–4).

---

16. *Spurgeon's Sermons*, vol. 1, *Heaven and Hell* (Grand Rapids: Baker, 1987), 297.

17. *Spurgeon's Sermons*, vol. 7, *The Wailing of Risca* (Grand Rapids: Baker, 1987), 333–34.

18. N.T. Wright, *Surprised by Hope: Rethinking Heaven, the Resurrection, and the Mission of the Church* (New York: HarperOne, 2008), 56.

19. Ironically, Jesus sent out the first heralds of His kingdom as sheep among wolves. They brought with them no weapon except God's word. They had to trust that God would build His kingdom by the gospel. See Goheen, *Light to the Nations*, 99.

Missional Christians Will Gather as Small Kingdom Communities
The small-group prayers of the early church were unquestionably eschatological. Believers appealed to God as king, imploring Him to move His kingdom forward through their witness (Acts 4:23–31; 12:12–19). Small group gatherings can also be a powerful way for church members to reach those who are not yet part of God's community. Orlando Saer writes, "It is the experience of countless small groups…that occasional…activities, meals, and other social events together provide the easiest and most natural opportunities to bring unbelievers into contact with a Christian community with the gospel message on their lips."[20]

Missional Christians Will Care for the Needy
Jesus's final public teaching prior to His crucifixion (according to Matthew) is a parable that ties together the doctrine of the last things and the mission of the church. According to Jesus those who will stand in the judgment are those who continued His mission of caring for the naked, the sick, and the imprisoned. Put more strongly, "the church fulfills its mission by taking to itself in mission, in Christ's name, for Christ's sake, the poverty, suffering, hunger, and need of men. Unless this is the situation, Matthew's description of the Christian community is the most searing piece of irony in the New Testament."[21] But let's not call

---

20. Orlando Saer, *Iron Sharpens Iron: Leading Bible-Oriented Small Groups that Thrive* (Fearn, Ross-shire, Scotland: Christian Focus, 2010), 22. See also Brad House, *Community: Taking Your Small Group Off Life Support* (Wheaton, Ill.: Crossway, 2011), 120–21; and William Boekestein, "10 Benefits of Church Small Groups," Core Christianity, March 19, 2018, https://corechristianity.com/resource-library/articles/10-benefits-of-church-small-groups. Of course for small groups to serve as useful mechanisms of gathering, they must be self-conscious about doing so. For a guide to organizing intentionally outward-oriented small groups, see C. John Miller, *Outgrowing the Ingrown Church* (Grand Rapids: Zondervan, 1986), 161–74.

21. Richard C. Oudersluys, "The Parable of the Sheep and Goats (Matthew 25:31–46): Eschatology and Mission, Then and Now," *Reformed Review* 26 (Spring 1973): 158.

it irony. Rather, let's prove true that "those who truly are watching for the return of their Lord will be most unceasing in their work of loving sympathy and relief, finding in this sorrowing, suffering world continual opportunities for manifesting a spirit of true charity, and unconsciously ministering to their Lord in the persons of those who are most in need."[22] Truly, with "deeds of love and mercy, the heav'nly kingdom comes."[23]

Works of mercy establish our credibility to speak to the deepest needs of the hurting and create a milieu in which to communicate the gospel's invitation to become new people. As God's people provide clothes for the naked and food for the hungry, so God provides forgiveness for sins, beauty for ashes, heaven for hell, wisdom for folly, glory for vanity.

Missional Christians Will Send and Support Missionaries
This side of glory, Jesus's assessment will never become obsolete: "The harvest truly is great, but the laborers are few; therefore pray the Lord of the harvest to send out laborers into His harvest" (Luke 10:2). Of course, Jesus didn't mean "just pray" for laborers; He calls for prayers as He is sending out laborers. So the church must prioritize the sending of ordained ministers[24] and other missionary helpers, and support them in such a way as to minimize their "worldly cares" and time spent raising funds.

---

22. Charles Erdman, *The Return of Christ*, 108.

23. *Trinity Psalter Hymnal*, 544.

24. "The church's missionary task is to preach the Word of God to the unconverted. When this task is to be performed beyond the field of an organized church, it is to be carried out by ministers of the Word set apart to this labor, who are called, supported and supervised by their Consistories. The churches should assist each other in the support of their missionaries." *Church Order of the United Reformed Churches in North America*, art. 47, accessed from http://www.urcna.org/1651/file_retrieve/23868. See also Romans 10:14–15.

Missional Christians Will Foster a Church Culture of Outreach
Outreach should never be simply a facet of church life but a central commitment. This means that every activity of the church should be tied to our calling to be a gathering community. This permeating missional calling should surely be taught. But teaching alone will not cultivate a generation of believers with the zeal and competency to be faithful witnesses. The church itself must become a culture of outreach. Church culture is critical because "culture predicts behavior. Embedded in the rites and rituals, culture takes a life of its own: It's just what an organization does."[25] As Peter Drucker said, "Culture eats strategy for breakfast."[26] Churches that are not incubators of outreach should hardly be surprised if less than 5 percent of Christians are personally involved in evangelism.[27]

Missional Christians Will Expect God to Bring in the Nations
We should believe that around the world God is bringing strangers into the covenants of promise (Eph. 2:12). We should also expect God to be doing so in our own churches. Paul assumed that "unbelievers" and "uninformed" persons would be present in church worship services (1 Cor. 14:23–25). So should we! On this basis Timothy Keller argues that while Christian worship services should be shaped by Scripture (and not by the preferences of believers or unbelievers) worship leaders should expect, and be intensely conscious of and sensitive to, the presence of unbelievers in the services (see Acts 2:37–41).[28] Faithfulness to our mission means that our worship services will be clear (but not simplistic),

---

25. Peter Greer and Chris Horst, *Mission Drift: The Unspoken Crisis Facing Leaders, Charities, and Churches* (Minneapolis: Bethany House, 2014), 149.

26. Quoted in Greer and Horst, *Mission Drift*, 149.

27. Based on information from George Barna, *Evangelism That Works* (Ventura, Calif.: Gospel Light, 1995), 23, and www.barna.org.

28. "Evangelistic Worship," accessed on May 2, 2017, from http://download.redeemer.com/pdf/learn/resources/Evangelistic_Worship-Keller.pdf.

hospitable (but not pandering), warm (but not soft), and beautiful (but not showy).

We also must insist on the declaration of a gospel that is robustly eschatological. The gospel declares that God is giving His people a kingdom and sovereignly drawing them (John 6:44) into His deep and rich plans. A humanly engineered and executed eschatology is utterly devoid of the gospel and, therefore, unable to promote the shalom that God promises. That gospel of Christ's finished propitiatory work, with all of its implications—an eschatological gospel focused on the hope-giving message that God is fully invested in His creation and that He is making all things new (Rev. 21:5)—is good news for believers and unbelievers.

William Manson sums up the mission of the church saying, "Its notes are hope and a sense of urgency."[29] If either ingredient, hope or urgency, is missing, Christian mission will fail to live up to the high calling of the mission of God. Where both are present, believers should prepare to watch God work.

---

29. Manson, "Mission and Eschatology," *International Review of Mission* 42, no. 168 (October 1953): 392.

Study Questions | Chapter 1

1. What is your interest level in the end times? What about the topic piques your interest?

2. Are there reasons that might incline you to not be interested in studying the end times?

3. What thoughts from this chapter have deepened your desire to better understand eschatology?

4. How do the following passages show God's will for us to develop an "apocalyptic spirituality," a spirituality that is shaped by a right reflection on the end times: 2 Corinthians 5:9–11; 1 Thessalonians 5:1–6; Hebrews 10:23–25; 2 Peter 3:8–14?

5. In a few sentences, articulate some of the possible end-times assumptions of a person who is not steeped in the doctrine of Scripture.

6. Reflect on a time when the promise of a deadline and subsequent judgment moved you to action. Was it a term paper, a final exam, tax day? How do these kinds of illustrations fall short of describing believers' anticipation of the last day?

7. When you think about the end of all things, do you tend to think more about how the end affects you in individual terms (death, glorification) or about the cosmic implications of the end of this present age?

8. How do individual and general eschatology balance each other?

Study Questions | Chapter 2

1. What is your impression of the ministry of the prophets and the parts of the Bible that they wrote? Does their message tend to resonate with you, or does it feel strangely inapplicable?

2. What is hermeneutics, and why is it important?

3. Reflect on some of the most important points of the creation-fall-redemption-restoration scheme of the story in Scripture. What benefits are there in seeing Scripture as a story?

4. How do the following Old Testament passages, and others that might come to your mind, help to contribute to a biblical eschatology: Job 19:25–27; Daniel 7:9–14; Joel 2:1–11?

5. Note some examples of symbolism in Revelation 1:9–16. Is it necessary for these symbols to be understood literally in order for them to powerfully communicate? What impression do these symbols give of the glorified Christ?

6. Is there biblical evidence that the Old Testament prophetic message is all about Jesus? If so, why did His own disciples, and so many people today, not use the prophets' message to trust in Christ?

7. Are there ways in which John's Revelation is susceptible to abuse?

8. What is the basic message of Revelation, and how does the book develop that message?

9. How does the message of Revelation comfort you?

Study Questions | Chapter 3

1. Are you, and those close to you, comfortable talking about death? If not, why not?

2. How does the ministry of Christ impact your view of death?

3. Can you remember a time that you grew in godliness by attending a funeral?

4. How would you advise those considering whether to take their young children with them to a funeral?

5. In John 11:32–44, how does Jesus model appropriate grief over death?

6. How do His words and actions (John 11:20–27) encourage hope in the shadow of death?

7. How has God healed you after the painful loss of a loved one?

8. How can a Christian rightly wrestle with the cremation option?

9. The chapter cautioned against the use of funeral eulogies. If given the appropriate context to comment on the life of a loved one, what kind of themes might you want to emphasize?

Study Questions | Chapter 4

1. Why does Paul warn against the philosophy, "Let us eat and drink, for tomorrow we die" (1 Cor. 15:32)?

2. In what ways do we feel pressure to live for today, forgetting about the age to come?

3. How can the human sense of eternity (Eccl. 3:11) be used as a way to communicate the gospel to our unbelieving friends?

4. Why might, according to Sinclair Ferguson, "the greatest heresy of the western world" be "the heresy that we are acceptable to God simply because we have died"?

5. Read Hebrews 4:1–10. Why is the word *today* so powerful in the passage?

6. How is it that believers and unbelievers can be both united and distinguished at death?

7. How might Christians so overly focus on the "gain" of dying that we eclipse the idea of anticipation in the intermediate state?

8. It is painful to reflect on the panicked state of unbelievers in sheol. Why might it be beneficial to do so?

Study Questions | Chapter 5

1. What can happen when the return of Christ is isolated from the biblical narrative?

2. Read Revelation 21:1–4, 22–27. How do these verses speak to the presence of God with His people and the centrality of the return of Christ?

3. Can you think of biblical texts or concepts that summarize the promise of the gospel as blessed presence with God?

4. Interact biblically and experientially with the following statement: Christ is not literally returning. The image of His return is simply meant to inspire zeal in fulfilling His ideals.

5. Why were Jesus's disciples troubled by His departure? (See John 14:1–6.) How does He comfort them in their sadness (John 14:15–18)?

6. What are some of the signs of Christ's return? Of what use are these signs to us?

7. The Nicene Creed says that Jesus "shall come again, with glory." What is the significance of the word *glory*?

Study Questions | Chapter 6

1. What does the word *millennium* mean? In general, how is the word used in Revelation 20?

2. What is premillennialism? What is postmillennialism?

3. What is amillennialism?

4. Summarize the dialogue in Matthew 12:25–30. How are Jesus's words encouraging?

5. Who are the souls who reign with Christ for a thousand years? What effect can this "great a cloud of witnesses" (Heb. 12:1) have on the church today?

6. In what sense do believers live and reign with Christ even prior to death? (See Rev. 1:6; Heidelberg Catechism 32.)

7. Does Revelation 20 seem to suggest a literal military battle between God's people and Gog and Magog? If not, what does this battle symbolize?

8. How does Revelation 20:1–10 exalt God and encourage God's people?

Study Questions | Chapter 7

1. What is notable about the data that indicates that people believe in the resurrection of Jesus but not in the resurrection of themselves?

2. Why is Paul so negative about a sort of Christianity *minus* the resurrection of the body? (See 1 Cor. 15:14–19, for example.)

3. Why do the biblical authors so closely connect the general resurrection with Jesus's resurrection? Note how they do so in texts like Romans 8:11; Philippians 3:21; 1 Peter 1:3; and 1 John 3:2.

4. Read 1 Corinthians 15:35–49 and interact with Paul's "seed" illustration.

5. How does this illustration support our understanding that resurrected bodies will be both similar to and different from our current bodies?

6. How do both the similarity and the dissimilarity encourage you?

7. Ponder this thought: "Church is an appointed gathering of named people in particular places who practice a life of resurrection in a world in which death gets the biggest headlines.... The practice of resurrection is an intentional, deliberate decision to believe and participate in resurrection *life,* life out of death, life that trumps death, life that is the last word, Jesus life."[1]

---

1. Eugene Peterson, *Practice Resurrection: A Conversation on Growing Up in Christ* (Grand Rapids: Eerdmans, 2010), 12.

Study Questions | Chapter 8

1. Do you sense that the final judgment is one of the least appealing traits of Christianity? Why or why not?

2. If only conceptually, what about the final judgment could be appealing even for non-Christians?

3. How do the following texts ground the final judgment in the moral lives of people: Matthew 25:31–46; John 5:27–29; 2 Peter 3:7?

4. How does the final judgment glorify Christ?

5. Jesus often directs the day of judgment as a warning against insincere religious people (cf. Matt. 10:5–15; 11:20–24; 12:33–37). What application can we glean from this?

6. How should believers face the prospect of being judged by Jesus?

7. How does the restoration of heaven and earth challenge previous notions about the new heaven and earth? What is appealing about a restoration (rather than an annihilation) of this present earth?

8. Reflect on some appropriate responses to the final judgment (e.g., trust God, be careful about judging others, live carefully before God's face).

Study Questions | Chapter 9

1. Is it okay to not like hell while at the same time accepting the biblical record of hell and its attendant responsibilities?

2. How might it be true that "imaginative, lurid, and eager descriptions of hell can needlessly hinder others from embracing the Bible and its Author"?

3. How can one reject a literal interpretation of the imagery of hell while still taking those images seriously?

4. Why is annihilationism so appealing? How would you critique this view?

5. How is hell consistent with God's perfect justice?

6. How is the doctrine of hell *not* to be used?

7. How can hell help us to fight against sin?

8. What does hell teach us about God?

9. How can hell deepen our love for Christ?

Study Questions | Chapter 10

1. Why does heaven seem strange, even unreal, to us? What are some of the dangers of such a view of heaven?

2. How does God's promise to bequeath land to the patriarchs (Gen. 17:8; Heb. 11:13) help us understand heaven (see Rom. 4:13)?

3. Read Isaiah 65:17–25 and reflect on the tangible descriptions of the new heaven and earth.

4. Why is a physical heaven so important to our hope of glory?

5. Have you ever faltered over the thought of heaven as unending worship? How would you help a believer who found such a prospect uninviting?

6. Christ is the second Adam (1 Cor. 15:45–49) who will return to reverse the curse invoked by Adam's sin. How are you encouraged by the thought of heaven as analogous to, but better than, pre-fall paradise?

7. Should we work for a sort of heaven on earth (see Matt. 6:10)?

8. What practical steps could you and your group take to better reflect the fellowship that believers will enjoy in heaven?

Study Questions | Chapter 11

1. The author writes: "Too often Christianity is seen simply as a means of escaping hell…. With such a view, virtually nothing else matters except 'going to heaven when I die.'" Interact with this thought.

2. Generally speaking, how is *kingdom* an "enlarging" word? How might it stand in contrast to an unbiblical individualism?

3. In telling the story of God's kingdom, what is meant by the following phrases: the kingdom *promised*, the kingdom *inaugurated*, the kingdom *realized*?

4. How does God's kingdom come on a personal, spiritual level?

5. How is this aspect of the kingdom bolstered by the promise of the perfected kingdom?

6. In these "perilous times" (2 Tim. 3:1) how are you encouraged by God's present reign over all things?

7. Read Matthew 6:25–34, with a focus on verses 33–34. How does Jesus contrast a life of kingdom seeking? What does this contrast teach us about a kingdom-seeking life?

8. What are some ways that your group can live as citizens of God's kingdom in promoting social justice (Luke 3:3–6) even as we wait for God to make every rough way smooth?

Study Questions | Chapter 12

1. How can Christ's perceived "slackness" at returning help us prioritize missions (see 2 Peter 3:8–9)?

2. Why is it important to understand the church as an organic continuity of Israel?

3. Note how the following passages demonstrate that Israel was expressly called to be a light to the nations: Genesis 12:1–3; Deuteronomy 10:19; Psalm 98:2–3; Isaiah 49:6; 60:2–3.

4. Is it true that "those who most eagerly look for the return of their Lord will be the most earnest in pressing for the accomplishment" of the Great Commission? (See Matt. 25:14–30.)

5. Why is a hopeful eschatology essential for missional living?

6. How can small groups help the church fulfill the Great Commission? How can your group be more intentionally missional?

7. Why is care for the needy a critical application of an eschatological missiology? How can your group more intentionally care for the needy?

8. Why is it important to expect God to gather the lost not only into *the* church but into *your* church?

Selected Bibliography

Alcorn, Randy. "C. S. Lewis on Heaven and the New Earth: God's Eternal Remedy to the Problem of Evil and Suffering." *Desiring God* (blog). September 28, 2013. http://www.desiringgod .org/messages/c-s-lewis-on-heaven-and-the-new-earth-god -s-eternal-remedy-to-the-problem-of-evil-and-suffering.

Bavinck, Herman. *The Last Things: Hope for This World and the Next.* Grand Rapids: Baker, 1996.

———. *Reformed Dogmatics.* Vol. 2, *God and Creation.* Grand Rapids: Baker Academic, 2004.

Bavinck, J. H. *An Introduction to the Science of Missions.* Philadelphia: Presbyterian and Reformed, 1960.

Baxter, Richard. *The Saints' Everlasting Rest* (Fearn, Ross-Shire, Scotland: Christian Focus, 1998).

Beeke, Joel. *Revelation.* Lectio Continua Expository Commentary on the New Testament. Grand Rapids: Reformation Heritage Books, 2016.

Bell, Rob. *Love Wins: A Book about Heaven, Hell, and the Fate of Every Person Who Ever Lived.* New York: HarperCollins, 2011.

Berkhof, Louis. *Principles of Biblical Interpretation.* Grand Rapids: Baker, 1950.

———. *Systematic Theology.* Grand Rapids: Eerdmans, 1939.

Blaising, Craig A., and Darrell L. Bock. *Progressive Dispensationalism.* Grand Rapids: BridgePoint, 2000.

Bloom, John. "Lord, Prepare Me to End Well." *Desiring God* (blog). February 28, 2017. http://www.desiringgod.org/articles/lord -prepare-me-to-end-well.

Boekestein, William. "All Israel Will Be Saved: Evaluating Paul's Hope for the Jewish People." *Puritan Reformed Journal* 10, no. 2 (July 2018): 31–44.

———. *Bible Studies on Mark*. Grand Rapids: Reformed Fellowship, 2016.

Boettner, Loraine. *Immortality*. Philadelphia: Presbyterian and Reformed, 1956.

Brakel, Wilhelmus à. *The Christian's Reasonable Service*. Vol 4. Grand Rapids: Reformation Heritage Books, 1995.

Brown, Michael Grant, and Zach Keele. *Sacred Bond: Covenant Theology Explored*. 2nd ed. Grand Rapids: Reformed Fellowship, 2017.

Calvin, John. *Commentary upon the Acts of the Apostles*. Edited by Henry Beveridge. Grand Rapids: Baker, 1989.

———. *Institutes of the Christian Religion*. 2 vols. Grand Rapids: Eerdmans, 1962.

Carson, D. A. *Basics for Believers: An Exposition of Philippians*. Grand Rapids: Baker Books, 2004.

Chan, Francis, and Preston Sprinkle. *Erasing Hell: What God Said about Eternity, and the Things We've Made Up*. Colorado Springs: David C. Cook, 2011.

Dennison, James T. Jr. *The Reformed Confessions of the 16th and 17th Centuries in English Translation*. 4 vols. Grand Rapids: Reformation Heritage Books, 2008–2014.

DeYoung, Kevin. "Heaven Is a World of Love." *Gospel Coalition* (blog). July 15, 2015. https://blogs.thegospelcoalition.org/kevindeyoung/2015/07/15/heaven-is-a-world-of-love/.

Donne, John. *Devotions upon Emergent Occasions* and *Death's Duel*. New York: Random House, 1999.

Doriani, Daniel M. *Getting the Message: A Plan for Interpreting and Applying the Bible*. Phillipsburg, N.J.: Presbyterian and Reformed, 1996.

Erdman, Charles. *The Return of Christ*. New York: George H. Doran, 1922.

George, Timothy. "Cremation Confusion: Is It Unscriptural for a Christian to Be Cremated?" *Christianity Today*, May 21, 2002: 66.

Goheen, Michael. *A Light to the Nations: The Missional Church and the Biblical Story*. Grand Rapids: Baker Academic, 2011.

Greer, Peter, and Chris Horst. *Mission Drift: The Unspoken Crisis Facing Leaders, Charities, and Churches*. Minneapolis: Bethany House, 2014.

Greidanus, Sidney. *The Modern Preacher and the Ancient Text: Interpreting and Preaching Biblical Literature*. Grand Rapids: Eerdmans, 1981.

Heide, Gale Z. "What Is New about the New Heaven and the New Earth? A Theology of Creation from Revelation 21 and 2 Peter 3." *Journal of the Evangelical Theological Society* 40, no. 1 (March 1997): 37–56.

Helm, Paul. *The Last Things: Death, Judgment, Heaven and Hell*. Edinburgh: Banner of Truth, 1989.

Hendriksen, William. *The Bible on the Life Hereafter*. Grand Rapids: Baker, 1959.

———. *The Gospel of Luke*. New Testament Commentary. Grand Rapids: Baker, 1978.

———. *More Than Conquerors: An Interpretation of the Book of Revelation*. Grand Rapids: Baker, 1998.

———. *Three Lectures on the Book of Revelation*. Grand Rapids: Zondervan, 1949.

Hodge, Charles. *Systematic Theology*. 2 vols. Grand Rapids: Eerdmans, 1975.

Hoekema, Anthony. *The Bible and the Future*. Grand Rapids: Eerdmans, 1994.

———. "Heaven Not Just an Eternal Day Off." *Christianity Today*, September 20, 1985: 18–19.

Hoeksema, Herman. *Behold He Cometh: An Exposition of the Book of Revelation*. Grand Rapids: Reformed Free Publishing Association, 1969.

Horton, Michael. *The Christian Faith*. Grand Rapids: Zondervan, 2011.

House, Brad. *Community: Taking Your Small Group Off Life Support*. Wheaton, Ill.: Crossway, 2011.

Hughes, Archibald. *A New Heaven and a New Earth*. London: Marshall, Morgan & Scott, 1958.

Hughes, P. E. *Interpreting Prophecy: An Essay in Biblical Perspective.* Grand Rapids: Eerdmans, 1976.

Jackson, Samuel Macauley, ed. *The New Schaff-Herzog Encyclopedia of Religious Knowledge.* New York: Funk and Wagnalls, 1908.

Johnson, Dennis. *The Triumph of the Lamb: A Commentary on Revelation.* Phillipsburg, N.J.: P&R, 2001.

Keller, Timothy. "Evangelistic Worship." Accessed on May 2, 2017 from http://download.redeemer.com/pdf/learn/resources/Evangelistic _Worship-Keller.pdf.

———. *The Prodigal God: Recovering the Heart of the Christian Faith.* New York: Penguin Group, 2008.

———. *The Reason for God: Belief in an Age of Skepticism.* New York: Penguin Group, 2008.

———. *The Songs of Jesus: A Year of Daily Devotions in the Psalms.* New York: Viking, 2015.

Kik, J. Marcellus. *An Eschatology of Victory.* Phillipsburg, N.J.: Presbyterian and Reformed, 1971.

Kuyper, Abraham. *In the Shadow of Death: Meditations for the Sick-Room and at the Death-Bed.* Audubon, N.J.: Old Paths, 1994.

Ladd, George Eldon. *A Commentary on the Revelation of John.* Grand Rapids: Eerdmans, 1972.

———. *The Presence of the Future: The Eschatology of Biblical Realism.* Grand Rapids: Eerdmans, 1974.

———. *A Theology of the New Testament.* Grand Rapids: Eerdmans, 1974.

Lewis, C. S. *The Problem of Pain.* The C. S. Lewis Signature Classics. New York: HarperCollins, 2017.

———. *Reflections on the Psalms.* Glasgow: Fontana Books, 1958.

Manson, William. "The Biblical Doctrine of Mission." *International Review of Mission* 42, no. 167 (July 1953): 257–65.

———. "Mission and Eschatology." *International Review of Mission* 42, no. 167 (October 1953): 390–97.

Martin, Ralph. *The Epistle of Paul to the Philippians: An Introduction and Commentary.* Tyndale New Testament Commentaries. Grand Rapids: Eerdmans, 1999.

McCartney, Dan, and Charles Clayton. *Let the Reader Understand: A Guide to Interpreting and Applying the Bible*. Phillipsburg, N.J.: P&R, 2002.

McGinn, Bernard, ed. *Apocalyptic Spirituality: Treatises and Letters of Lactantius, Adso of Montier-en-Der, Joachim of Fiore, the Franciscan Spiritualists, Savonarola*. Classics of Western Spirituality: A Library of the Great Spiritual Masters. Mahwah, N.J.: Paulist Press, 1979.

Melloh, John Allyn. "Homily or Eulogy? The Dilemma of Funeral Preaching." *Worship* 67 (November 1993): 502–18.

Middleton, J. Richard. *A New Heaven and a New Earth: Reclaiming Biblical Eschatology*. Grand Rapids: Baker Academic, 2014.

Miller, C. John. *Outgrowing the Ingrown Church*. Grand Rapids: Zondervan, 1986.

Murray, John. *The Imputation of Adam's Sin*. Phillipsburg, N.J.: Presbyterian and Reformed, 1959.

Newbigin, Lesslie. *The Household of God: Lectures on the Nature of the Church*. New York: Friendship Press, 1954.

Orr, James, gen. ed. *The International Standard Bible Encyclopedia*. Grand Rapids: Eerdmans, 1952.

Oudersluys, Richard C. "The Parable of the Sheep and Goats (Matthew 25:31–46): Eschatology and Mission, Then and Now." *Reformed Review* 26 (Spring 1973): 151–61.

Packer, J. I. "Evangelical Annihilationism in Review." *Reformation & Revival Magazine* 6, no. 2 (Spring 1997): 37–52.

———. *Evangelism and the Sovereignty of God*. Downers Grove, Ill.: InterVarsity Press, 1961.

Peterson, Eugene. *Practice Resurrection: A Conversation on Growing Up in Christ*. Grand Rapids: Eerdmans, 2010.

Piper, John. "Don't Be Anxious, Lay up Treasure in Heaven, Part 1." *Desiring God* (blog). March 2, 2003. http://www.desiringgod .org/messages/dont-be-anxious-lay-up-treasure-in-heaven -part-1.

The Psalter. Grand Rapids: Reformation Heritage Books, 1999.

Psalter Hymnal. Grand Rapids: Board of Publications of the Christian Reformed Church, 1976.

Ramm, Bernard. *Protestant Biblical Interpretation*. 3rd rev. ed. Grand Rapids: Baker, 1970.

Ridderbos, Herman. *The Coming of the Kingdom*. Philadelphia: Presbyterian and Reformed, 1962.

Riddlebarger, Kim. *A Case for Amillennialism: Understanding the End Times*. Grand Rapids: Baker Books, 2013.

Ryken, Philip Graham. *City on a Hill: Reclaiming the Biblical Pattern for the Church in the 21st Century*. Chicago: Moody, 2003.

Ryrie, Charles. *Dispensationalism Today*. Chicago: Moody, 1965.

Saer, Orlando. *Iron Sharpens Iron: Leading Bible-Oriented Small Groups That Thrive*. Fearn, Ross-shire, Scotland: Christian Focus, 2010.

Shaeffer, Francis. *Pollution and the Death of Man: The Christian View of Ecology*. Wheaton, Ill.: Tyndale House, 1970.

Thomas, Robert L. "The Hermeneutics of Progressive Dispensationalism." *The Master's Seminary Journal* 6, no. 2 (Spring 1995): 79–95.

Trinity Hymnal. Suwanee, Ga.: Great Commission, 1990.

Trinity Psalter Hymnal. Willow Grove, Pa.: Trinity Psalter Hymnal Joint Venture, 2018.

Turretin, Francis. *Institutes of Elenctic Theology*. Vol 3. Phillipsburg, N.J.: P&R, 1997.

Venema, Cornel. *Christ and the Future: The Bible's Teaching about the Last Things*. Edinburgh: Banner of Truth, 2008.

Vos, Geerhardus. *Redemptive History and Biblical Interpretation: The Shorter Writings of Geerhardus Vos*. Edited by Richard B. Gaffin Jr. Phillipsburg, N.J.: Presbyterian and Reformed, 1980.

Waldner, Mike M. "Christian Mission in Eschatological Perspective: Promoting the Dynamic of Eschatology for Missionary Motivation." DMiss diss., Fuller Theological Seminary, School of World Mission, 1987.

Wright, N. T. *Surprised by Hope: Rethinking Heaven, the Resurrection, and the Mission of the Church*. New York: HarperOne, 2008.